Connecting Across Cultures

Connecting Across Cultures

The Helper's Toolkit

PAMELA A. HAYS, PhD

Los Angeles | London | New Delhi
Singapore | Washington DC

Los Angeles | London | New Delhi
Singapore | Washington DC

FOR INFORMATION:

SAGE Publications, Inc.
2455 Teller Road
Thousand Oaks, California 91320
E-mail: order@sagepub.com

SAGE Publications Ltd.
1 Oliver's Yard
55 City Road
London EC1Y 1SP
United Kingdom

SAGE Publications India Pvt. Ltd.
B 1/I 1 Mohan Cooperative Industrial Area
Mathura Road, New Delhi 110 044
India

SAGE Publications Asia-Pacific Pte. Ltd.
3 Church Street
#10-04 Samsung Hub
Singapore 049483

Senior Executive Editor: Kassie Graves
Editorial Assistant: Elizabeth Luizzi
Production Editor: Libby Larson
Copy Editor: Laurie Pitman
Typesetter: C&M Digitals (P) Ltd.
Proofreader: Theresa Kay
Indexer: Diggs Publication Services
Cover Designer: Michael Dubowe
Marketing Manager: Lisa Sheldon Brown
Permissions Editor: Adele Hutchinson

Printed in the United States of America

Library of Congress Cataloging-in-Publication Data

Hays, Pamela A.

Connecting across cultures: the helper's toolkit/Pamela A Hays.

p. cm.
Includes bibliographical references and index.

ISBN 978-1-4522-1791-8 (pbk.)

1. Multiculturalism. 2. Culture.
3. Interpersonal relations. I. Title.

HM1271.H397 2013
305.8—dc23   2012016270

This book is printed on acid-free paper.

12 13 14 15 16 10 9 8 7 6 5 4 3 2 1

Brief Contents

Detailed Contents

Acknowledgments

This book is a product of all the expertise and insider knowledge so generously shared with me over the years by my friends, family members, students, colleagues, and teachers. I am very grateful to my writing buddy, Mary Ann Boyle, and to the following family members and friends for their support and helpful feedback on the manuscript: Hugh and Marjorie Hays, Libby Tisdell, Carolyn Kenny, Paul Landen, Miguel Gallardo, Josephine Johnson, and Linda Mona. I also appreciate Brad Klontz's encouragement. I am especially grateful to my husband, Robert McCard, for his unwavering support, encouragement, and helpful feedback. And I would like to thank the SAGE staff and reviewers, especially senior acquisitions editor Kassie Graves.

Introduction

Diversity may be the hardest thing for a society to live with and perhaps the most dangerous thing for a society to be without.

—William Sloane Coffin, Jr.[1]

Building and sustaining relationships can be challenging, and the more diverse the world becomes, the greater the challenge. *Connecting Across Cultures: The Helper's Toolkit* focuses on the information helping professionals need. With fun exercises, helpful suggestions, straightforward strategies, and realistic case examples, you will learn the following:

- Push-button words and phrases that can unintentionally offend and preferable alternatives
- Verbal and nonverbal communication strategies that build respect
- How to think about values in ways that minimize conflict
- In-the-moment steps for defusing defensiveness
- How to create a positive connection despite the challenges involved

Because good relationships are essential for success in human services, health care, education, and counseling, this learning will increase your effectiveness and success at work. And because cross-cultural relationships involve all the usual relationship challenges plus the extra-difficult ones, what you learn in this book will help you with all your relationships.

---

[1]www.storiesfortrainers.com. Retrieved 12/30/11.

1

Diversity Is Unavoidable, and *That's a Good Thing*

Great achievements are not born from a single vision but from the combination of many distinctive viewpoints. Diversity challenges assumptions, opens minds, and unlocks our potential to solve any problems we may face.

—Source unknown[1]

B ob was living and teaching in a Siberian Yup'ik[2] village on Saint Lawrence Island, off the west coast of Alaska. The Siberian Yup'ik people are known for exceptional survival skills and awareness of the environment that help them to survive in an extreme climate. Listening, observing, and silence are highly valued, which makes sense when you consider that talking, loud noises, and fast movements scare away the fish and animals on which the people depend. Bob is a friendly person and throughout the day, whenever he passed one of the 33 students in the small school, he would always say "good morning" or "hi." One day one of his students said to him with

---

[1]Retrieved from http://multiracialfamily.org/2011/07/24/quote-great-achievements-are-not-born-from-a-single-vision/

[2]Pronounced Yoo-pik.

genuine curiosity, "Why do you [White] guys say hi so much? Once is enough." From the Siberian Yup'ik perspective, one hello per day was sufficient.

When I asked Bob how he responded to the student's question, he said it caught him off guard, but after that he made an effort to say hello only once each day to the student. He confessed that he continued to say hello several times to all the other students because it was ingrained in him as polite behavior.

I call Bob's experience of surprise at learning a totally new perspective the *aha!* experience. The thought that often accompanies such an experience is, "Wow, I never thought of it that way." Because people often assume that their own culture, beliefs, and ways are the best and only ways, the *aha!* experience can be unsettling and even painful. But if we avoid defensiveness and stay open to new ideas, the *aha!* experience can change our assumptions and behavior in ways that facilitate our relationships, broaden our perspectives, and enrich our lives. And much of the time, this learning can be fun.

Consider this: Have you ever had an *aha!* experience? Did it change your behavior or perspective?

❖ YOUR LIFE IS MULTICULTURAL, EVEN IF YOU DON'T KNOW IT

The world is in the midst of a multicultural revolution that touches everyone and offers possibilities for a richer, more interesting, and sustainable future. For example, in today's multicultural America, people of Latino, Asian, Native, Middle Eastern, Pacific Island, and African heritage make up over one third of the country.[3] Approximately 381 languages are spoken or signed.[4] Religious minorities include 2.6 million Jews, 1.3 million Muslims, 1 million Buddhists, and half a million Hindus.[5] People who identify as LGBT[6]

---

[3]U.S. Census Bureau. (2011). *2010 shows America's diversity* (American Community Survey). Retrieved from http://2010.census.gov/news/releases/operations/cb11-cn125.html

[4]U.S. Census Bureau. (2005–2009). *New Census Bureau report analyzes nation's linguistic diversity* (American Community Survey). Retrieved from www.census.gov/newsroom/releases/archives/american_community_survey_acs/cb10-cn58.html

are gaining increasing visibility, and approximately 19% of Americans have disabilities.[7] Generational differences cross all of these groups, as the average age of Americans increases, and 13% of Americans are now older adults.[8]

Consider this: In today's issue of your local newspaper, count how many articles are reporting on a cross-cultural conflict, cultural event, or person of a minority culture (i.e., defined broadly to include ethnic, racial, religious, and sexual minorities and people with disabilities). Are you surprised by the number?

To give you an idea of the positive possibilities all this diversity brings, consider some of the creations, solutions, and contributions of diverse minority cultures (i.e., ones you may have taken for granted or assumed were European American):

1. Healing practices such as Chinese acupuncture, tai chi, and chi gong; Buddhist meditation and mindfulness practices; and East Indian Ayurvedic medicine and yoga

2. Knowledge used to understand the impact of humans on the environment and develop pollution prevention strategies (e.g., Iñuit and Iñupiaq[9] elders' firsthand observations of the effects of global warming on ice, habitats, and animal populations)

3. Survival knowledge held by many Indigenous people of medicinal plants, hunting, fishing, farming, and navigation

---

[5]*American religion identification survey.* (2008). Retrieved from http://commons .trincoll.edu/aris/6.

[6]Acronym for people who identify as lesbian, gay, bisexual, or transgender.

[7]U.S. Census Bureau. (2000). 20th anniversary of Americans with Disabilities Act. Retrieved from www.census.gov/newsroom/releases/archives/facts_ for_features_special_editions/cb10-ff13.html

[8]U.S. Census Bureau. (2010). Older Americans month. Retrieved from www .census.gov/newsroom/releases/archives/facts_for_features_special_editions/ cb10-ff06.html

[9]Pronounced Ih-nyoo-it and Ih-nyoo'-pee-ak.

4. Music and musical instruments, including Caribbean reggae, Algerian rai, Tuva throat singing, the Aboriginal didgeridoo, Hindu chants, and African American jazz, blues, and rap

5. Artwork such as Navajo tapestries, South American pottery, Alaska Native ivory carvings, African wood carvings, and Chinese calligraphy

6. Dance, including Hawaiian hula, Louisiana Creole zydeco, African American break dancing, Latin American tango and salsa, and AXIS—the collaborative dance of people with and without disabilities

7. Diverse languages that include words for concepts that do not exist in all cultures and find expression in, for example, Arabic poetry, Japanese haiku, Native storytelling, Greek mythology, and Russian literature

8. Innovations such as the Chinese inventions of the clock, paper money, movable type printing, fireworks, and compass; Arab inventions of the decimal system, Arabic numerals, the symbol for zero, artificial insemination for breeding horses, and the mechanical calendar; the Persian invention of sugar extraction; the Aztec invention of hydroponics (plants grown without soil)

9. Unique foods, herbs, spices, and cooking techniques, including Japanese sushi, African couscous, Chinese stir-fry, East Indian samosas, American Indian fry bread, Tibetan lentil soup, and Turkish baklava

10. Clothing and fabrics that are beautiful, practical, inspirational, and/or derived from Indigenous plants and materials—for example, the African caftan, Hawaiian muumuu, Indian sari, embroidered Mexican dresses, colorful Indonesian fabrics, and the Gay Pride flag

11. Architecture—for example, domes that naturally cool homes in North Africa and Spain; Japanese gardens and pagodas; beautiful and inspiring mosques, synagogues, cathedrals, and Buddhist and Hindu temples; and the East Indian Taj Mahal

12. Forms of celebration, including Disability Pride parades, Chinese New Year, Mardi Gras, the Muslim celebration of Eid at the end of Ramadan, Mexican fiesta, African American Kwanzaa, Jewish bar mitzvah and bat mitzvah, Gay Pride parades, and diverse wedding rituals

❖ WHAT YOU DON'T KNOW *CAN* HURT YOU

Many White people believe that they do not have a culture, perhaps because when you are immersed in the dominant European American culture, it is difficult to see its influence. Think of asking a fish to describe how it is affected by water, when the fish has never been out of water. Perceiving cultural influences is easier when there is some sort of contrast. For many European Americans, this contrast and the first recognition of having a culture comes when visiting another country. But for members of minority groups, being in the minority brings continual awareness of one's culture and minority status.

With or without awareness, culture influences us all. And as diversity increases, so do misunderstandings and conflicts. Well-intentioned members of dominant groups are often unaware of the ways in which their language and behavior communicate bias. Take the following quiz and see if you can figure out what the dominant-culture member did that offended the other person.

EXERCISE 1.1

Awareness Quiz

Situation 1

Not long after she was hired, a 50-year-old European American manager named Sharon[10] noticed the tension between Linda (a White employee) and Rhadiya (the department's only African American and only Muslim). Sharon initiated separate conversations with each woman to look for a way to facilitate that person's working relationship. Rhadiya told Sharon that she felt less valued by the department and gave examples of team meetings in which she had expressed her opinion and Linda ignored her. She acknowledged that this had occurred only with Linda but felt irritated that none of the other White employees seemed to notice or care. When Sharon talked with Linda, Linda became defensive and denied any negative feelings or disrespectful behavior on her part. Sharon felt concerned about the situation so she asked Rhadiya if she would be interested in making a presentation to the department on cultural issues ("a sort of minitraining to increase our awareness," she said). To Sharon's surprise, Rhadiya appeared irritated and said she had no interest in doing such a presentation.

(Continued)

---

[10]All examples are composites with pseudonyms.

(Continued)

Question: Why was Rhadiya offended?

Answer: Rhadiya took Sharon's request as evidence of Sharon's unwillingness to take the time to learn about African Americans and Muslims or find a diversity expert to train the department. Rhadiya resented the implication that it was her responsibility to educate her White coworkers. She knew from experience that talking about race and religion with European American non-Muslims often elicits defensiveness, and to conduct such a training would place her in a vulnerable position. A defensive reaction already appeared to be occurring with Linda's denial that there was any problem, and based on the other White employees' lack of reaction, Rhadiya guessed that she could not count on their support. Although Sharon recognized the need for the White employees to be more culturally sensitive, by asking Rhadiya to do the training, she was putting the problem back on Rhadiya, reinforcing Linda's implication that "*Rhadiya* is the one with the problem, not me."

Situation 2

On the first day of a college social studies class, the topic of gay marriage came up. The teacher (who identified as heterosexual) was aware that there were two students who identified as gay and made the statement "No one should be discriminated against because of his or her sexual preference." After class, the teacher moved toward the two students (who were sitting together) in order to make a personal connection with them. As they stood up, they nodded at her to acknowledge her presence but then turned away and quickly left. It was clear they did not want to talk with her, which left her feeling hurt and confused.

Question: What did the teacher do or say that offended the students?

Answer: The teacher's use of the term sexual *preference,* rather than sexual *orientation,* assumed that a person chooses to be gay, with the implication that one can choose not to be. This assumption of choice is commonly used by antigay groups to justify discrimination. Although the teacher may have been open to feedback about her language, she did not have the opportunity because her words offended the students who then avoided her. In addition, she may have embarrassed the students when she moved toward them immediately after the discussion, especially if they were not open about their sexual orientation in this setting. Her move toward them also assumed that they were the only students who identified as gay or lesbian, which may not have been the case.

Situation 3

A man in his late 50s was exiting an elevator at the same time as a woman who was using a wheelchair. As the woman began to move her wheelchair forward, the man said, "Oh, let me help you" and quickly reached for the handlebars to give her a push. The woman stated firmly, "Please don't touch my wheelchair." He was surprised, then felt irritated because as he later told a friend, "I was just trying to help. A person can't even be polite anymore."

Question: What did the man do wrong?

Answer: The man was unaware of social norms from the perspective of a person with a disability. For people who have disabilities, assistive animals and devices (e.g., wheelchairs, canes, and walkers) function as extensions of the person's body. As the psychologist Rhoda Olkin[11] notes, you would never touch a person's legs without asking, so you wouldn't want to touch someone's assistive device or assistance animal without permission. By reaching for her wheelchair handlebars, the man was violating the woman's personal space and taking control of her mobility without asking if this was what she wanted.

Situation 4

Mark came to his college counseling center asking for help in figuring out what jobs to apply for after graduation. In response to the young White counselor's questions about Mark's background, Mark said his mother was Iñupiaq (Alaska Native) and father White (Russian/European American). After his parents divorced, he and his older siblings took turns staying with their father in the city and their mother in a rural area. When he was 18, his father died, and he decided to stay with his mother for a semester, during which time, his maternal grandparents both died. Mark became tearful when he said this and changed the subject back to his career search. The counselor was familiar with the many losses experienced by Alaska Native people and told Mark that he could see Mark had experienced many losses in his life and might need an opportunity to grieve more fully. He added that counseling might be of assistance. At his encouragement, Mark made another appointment, but the next week, Mark did not appear, and the counselor did not hear from him again.

Question: Why didn't Mark return?

Answer: The counselor had a limited knowledge of Alaska Native cultures, and the little he knew was from a dominant cultural lens that focused on negatives. He had heard of alcoholism, domestic violence, and historical oppression, but he did not know of the many positive, healthy parts of Alaska Native cultures. If he had had a more holistic understanding of Native cultures and more experience with Native people, he could have seen

---

[11]Olkin, R. (1999). *What psychotherapists should know about disability.* New York: Guilford.

Mark's cultural heritage as a source of strength and support. If he had asked questions from this positive perspective, he would have learned that Mark belonged to a Native dance group, which was a source of pride, fun, and social support; that he was a role model for his younger nieces and nephews; and that his extended family and church provided plenty of emotional, social, and physical support. Mark had many opportunities to grieve with people who knew his father and grandparents well and did not need a counselor for help in coping with these feelings.

Although all of the dominant-culture members above were well-intentioned, their good intentions did not automatically eliminate their biases, and these biases led to hurtful mistakes.

Consider this: Have you ever had an experience similar to one above where something went wrong and you didn't know what? Were you able to keep a connection with the person?

Most of us have learned how to interact with others largely by trial and error, and in the process, we make mistakes. *Relationship* mistakes are difficult to correct because the people who could give us feedback often pull away and stop interacting with us. When culture is added to the mix, relationship mistakes become more complex and difficult. Culture is like an iceberg; in the midst of all this complexity, it is the enormous part you can't see and risk crashing into if you don't know it's there.[12]

If one is a member of a minority group, relationship mistakes may be experienced as what psychologist Derald Wing Sue calls *microaggressions*—verbal or behavioral insults from members of the dominant culture.[13] When the action is unintentional, the dominant member may be oblivious to the pain his or her comment or action has caused the minority member. If the dominant member does become aware, he or she often feels embarrassed and becomes defensive. Meanwhile, the minority member is left feeling hurt, confused, and sometimes angry.

[12]Comas-Díaz, L. (2011). *Multicultural care: A clinician's guide to cultural competence.* Washington, DC: American Psychological Association.

[13]Sue, D. W., Capodilupo, C. M., Torino, G. C., Bucceri, J. M., Holder, A. M. B., Nadal, K. L., & Esquilin, M. (2007). Racial microaggressions in everyday life. *American Psychologist, 62,* 271–286.

In her essay "My Black Skin Makes My White Coat Vanish," Dr. Mana Lumumba-Kasongo describes her ongoing experience with microaggressions related to dominant cultural stereotypes:

> Over the years, the inability of patients and others to believe that I am a doctor has left me utterly demoralized. . . . How can it be that with all the years of experience I have, all the procedures I've performed and all the people I've interacted with in emergency situations, I still get what I call "the look?" . . . I walk in the room and introduce myself then wait for the patient—whether he or she is black, white or Asian—to steal glances at the ID card that is attached to my scrubs or white coat. (I've thought of having it changed to read something like: *"It's true. I'm a real doctor. Perhaps you've seen a black one on TV?"*)[14]

Consider this: Have you ever experienced or unintentionally performed a microaggression? Did you realize that it was a microaggression at the time? How did you feel afterward?

Hidden Information

Because the dominant culture is so dominant, minority perspectives are often outvoted, hidden from, or ignored by the dominant culture, and the identities of successful members of minority cultures are overlooked or de-emphasized. For example, did you know that the following individuals are Latino?

- Musicians Joan Baez, Gloria Estefan, Linda Ronstadt, Mariah Carey, opera star Plácido Domingo, Cuban-born Desi Arnaz of *I Love Lucy*, Carlos Santana, Trini Lopez, teenage group Menudo, and Jon Secada

- Actors Martin Sheen (born Ramón Estevez), Rita Hayworth (born Rita Cansino), Cuban-born Andy García, Mexican-born Anthony Quinn, Raquel Welch (born Raquel Welch Tejada), Puerto Rican Rita Moreno, and Raul Julia

- Baseball player Roberto Walker Clemente, golfer Lee Trevino, tennis star Rosemary Casals, and former Raiders quarterback and coach Tom Flores

---

[14]Lumumba-Kasongo, M. (2006, April 3). My Black skin makes my White coat vanish. *Newsweek, 147*(14), 20.

- Former Housing and Urban Development Secretary Henry Cisneros; former New Mexico governor and presidential candidate Bill Richardson; Head of the White House Office of Public Liaison under President Carter, Linda Chavez; and first Latina U.S. Surgeon General under President Bush, Antonia Novello[15]

Similarly, mainstream history books rarely mention the enormous agricultural, scientific, and medical contributions by African Americans to the United States before, during, and after slavery. The U.S. Patent Office's refusal to grant patents to slaves (which would have countered the view of African Americans as incapable) persisted despite the large number of inventions by African Americans.

These African American inventors included Elijah McCoy, who developed the automatic engine lubricator; so many people made cheap imitations of his invention that would-be purchasers coined the phrase "Is this the real McCoy?" Garrett Augustus Morgan invented the gas mask in 1912, which saved the lives of hundreds of soldiers during World War I. Postal worker Shelby Davidson invented the adding machine; Frederick McKinley Jones, the portable X-ray machine; and Lloyd Augusta Hall, curing salts that revolutionized the meatpacking industry. Dr. Mae Jamison was a pioneering astronaut who flew on the shuttle *Endeavor*; Dr. Lewis Wright developed the neck brace; Dr. William Hinton developed the Davies-Hinton test for syphilis detection; and Dr. Samuel Kountz founded the largest kidney transplant research center and made history by transplanting a kidney from mother to daughter.[16]

The scientific and medical contributions of Arab and Muslim cultures are similarly unrecognized by the dominant European American culture. Between the 9th and 13th centuries (known as the Golden Era of Islam) an enormous number of inventions and cultural developments took place as the Arabs spread Islam beyond Arabia. Arabs developed a hospital routine that is still practiced today including formal registration of patients, case notes taken on daily morning rounds, and medical examinations with pulse taking, tapping to sound out internal organs, questioning the patient, and examination of the color and feel of the skin, type and depth of breathing, and the patient's

[15]Novas, H. (1994). *Everything you need to know about Latino history*. New York: Penguin.

[16]Stewart, J. C. (1996). *1001 things you should know about African American history*. New York: Broadway Books.

urine. At a time when surgeons were considered butchers in Europe, Arabs were using anesthesia for surgery and had a formal text describing routine surgical procedures, including catheterization of a male patient.

The surgical manual developed by al-Zahrawi (AD 1000) was still in use by Oxford's medics during the 18th century, and Al-Majusi described a variety of contraceptive methods that were used in the Middle East for more than 1,000 years. Before Jenner developed the cowpox vaccine, the European Lady Montague learned the technique of smallpox vaccination from the Muslims (specifically the Turks), which she then brought to England. And long before Freud developed his talking cure, Al-Razi wrote of the *ilaj-il-nafsani,* a talking treatment for the psyche.[17]

Although one can find information *about* minority perspectives in the mainstream media, the bulk of this information is written, directed, and produced by members of the dominant culture—people who are predominantly European American, middle class, heterosexual, nondisabled, monolingual, and of Christian heritage. Because such information is filtered through a dominant cultural lens, it is skewed in favor of the dominant culture. For this reason, it is not enough to simply be open to new perspectives. True cross-cultural understanding requires extra work—looking for and learning the culture-specific information and communication skills necessary for relationship success.

EXERCISE 1.2

Expanding Your View

Make a list of at least 10 positive minority cultural influences that affect or could affect your life. If you have difficulty finding influences, search online using the name of a minority culture and positive terms such as *Muslim/Islamic inventions, discoveries; African American accomplishments, innovations; lesbian/gay contributions, community building.* For example, if you do a search regarding *well-known successful people with disabilities,* you will find information on people with disabilities who are successful actors and

(Continued)

---

[17]Ashrif, S. (1987). Eurocentrism and myopia in science teaching. *Multicultural Teaching, 5,* 28–30.

(Continued)

musicians (Tom Cruise, Stevie Wonder, Ray Charles, Marlee Matlin, Robin Williams, Beethoven); professional athletes (Magic Johnson, Jim Abbott); inventors (Albert Einstein, Thomas Edison, Alexander Graham Bell); and political leaders (Winston Churchill, Franklin D. Roosevelt, Kansas Senator Bob Dole).[18] Use this information to think about how these individuals may have influenced you or created influences that positively affect your life or perspective.

[18]Palsson, J. (2008, December).10 famous people with disabilities. *ArticleDoctor.* Retrieved from www.articledoctor.com/disability/10-famous-people-disabilities -581

2

The Starting Place

Knowing Who You Are

Until we can understand the assumptions in which we are drenched we cannot know ourselves.

—Adrienne Rich

Take a minute to think about how you identify yourself with the following exercise. Fill in the blanks of the statement "I am _____" with whatever words you use to describe who you are. For example, I am *a woman, Jewish, an elder, father of an adopted child, a soldier, Japanese American, middle class, gay, a person with a disability, Buddhist, an American, Spanish-speaking, a single mother, an immigrant,* and so on. Use as many blanks as you need.

As the multicultural expert Beverly Greene points out, all of the following individuals are Christians: members of the Ku Klux Klan, Nazis and their sympathizers, Martin Luther King Jr., Condoleezza Rice, and George Bush—but this tells us little about Christians or Christianity. As she notes, Martin Luther King Jr. had more in common with Gandhi than with any of these Christians, but Gandhi was Hindu.[1]

---

[1]Greene, B. (2009). The use and abuse of religious beliefs in dividing and conquering between socially marginalized groups: The same-sex marriage debate. *American Psychologist, 64,* 698–709.

EXERCISE 2.1

Who Am I?

I am_____.   I am_____.

I am_____.   I am_____.

I am_____.   I am_____.

I am_____.   I am_____.

Now look at your self-description. If you were able to fill in several of the blanks, apparently you identify yourself in many ways. Most of us think of ourselves as complex and interesting people. We would be reluctant to say that a sole characteristic defines who we are.

In contrast, we often think of other people in singular terms, particularly members of groups with whom we have little experience. This narrow perception of others limits our ability to accurately understand and connect with those we perceive as different from ourselves. An example includes assuming that a person's identity as Muslim explains everything about him—who he is, what he values, his political and religious beliefs, and so on.

No one identity can summarize the wholeness of any given person. Just as we perceive our own richness, recognizing the richness in others is the first step toward understanding and connecting. When we begin to see, or better yet, *look for* this richness, a world of difference and possibilities opens.

The ADDRESSING Culture Sketch

To understand how cultural influences shape what you think, feel, and do, let's start with an exercise I call the ADDRESSING Culture Sketch. The acronym ADDRESSING stands for nine cultural influences that affect us all. As you can see in Table 2.1 each of the ADDRESSING influences has a dominant cultural group and a nondominant (minority) group associated with it.

Defining a person as belonging to a dominant or minority group can be complicated, because what constitutes dominant or minority status depends on the situation. In general, a dominant group is one that has privileges, power, and resources that minority groups do not. Many times the dominant group is a numerical majority (e.g., White people in the United States) but not always. For example, women in the United States are considered a minority because women are underrepresented in positions of power, status, and high pay.

Complicating the distinction further is that many people belong to *both* minority and dominant groups—for example, a biracial woman whose father is African American and mother European American or a European American man who has a disability. Within an individual, some dominant influences are more powerful than others and can override minority influences to determine one's status. For instance, older European Americans generally experience lower status in the United States because of their age, even though they are White. However, if that older White person is male and wealthy, he will experience especially high status. Wealthy and White trump old age.

Table 2.1   ADDRESSING Cultural Influences[2]

Cultural Influences	Dominant Group	Nondominant/Minority Group
Age and generational influences	Young/middle aged adults	Children, older adults
Developmental disabilities & other Disabilities	Nondisabled people	People with cognitive, sensory, physical, and/or psychiatric disabilities
Religion and spirituality	Christian & secular	Muslims, Jews, Hindus, Buddhists, & other minority religions
Ethnic and racial identity	European Americans	Asian, South Asian, Latino, Pacific Island, African, Arab, African American, & Middle Eastern people
Socioeconomic status	Upper & middle class	People of lower status by occupation, education, income, or inner-city/rural habitat
Sexual orientation	Heterosexuals	People who identify as gay, lesbian, or bisexual

(Continued)

[2]Adapted from Hays, P. A. (2008). *Addressing cultural complexities in practice: Assessment, diagnosis, and therapy.* Washington, DC: American Psychological Association.

Table 2.1   (Continued)

Cultural Influences	Dominant Group	Nondominant/Minority Group
Indigenous heritage	European Americans	American Indians, Iñuit, Alaska Natives, Métis, Native Hawaiians
National origin	U.S.-born Americans	Immigrants, refugees, & international students
Gender	Men	Women and people who identify as transgender

As Table 2.1 indicates, *A* stands for "*A*ge and generational influences," including not just your chronological age but any cultural influences that have profoundly affected members of your generation. If you are an American in your late 50s, this could include post–World War II economic prosperity, Vietnam War protests, drugs, rock 'n roll music, and the civil rights and women's movements, to name just a few. In contrast, if you are in your early 20s, your generation has been strongly affected by computer technology, social media, widespread use of psychotropic medications, the economic downturn, and unemployment. Granted, older people have also been affected by these more recent influences; however, younger people have never experienced life without them.

Generational influences can also include generational *roles* that have shaped who you are. For example, being an oldest son may have contributed to your particular opportunities and choices in ways that are quite different from those of a youngest daughter. Other roles that are important for many people include those of parent, grandparent, aunt, or uncle.

In some cultures, particular generational roles carry responsibilities that are different from those of the dominant culture. For example, in the traditional Alaska Native culture of the Tlingit, the maternal uncle takes responsibility for rearing a woman's son, even when the woman lives with the son's father. In the dominant European American culture, children and older people are commonly considered minorities, although in many cultures, older adults are accorded higher status and are the dominant group.

DD stands for "*D*evelopmental disabilities" (e.g., disabilities related to Down syndrome or fetal alcohol spectrum disorder) and "other *D*isabilities" (e.g., those acquired at birth or later in life or secondary to chronic health conditions). Minority groups include people who have cognitive, sensory, physical, and/or psychiatric disabilities.

If you do not have a disability and belong to the dominant group of nondisabled people, this influence is a reminder of the cognitive, sensory, physical, and psychological abilities you do have, and their influence on you. Like the fish in water, if you have never had a disability or been a caregiver for someone who has, you probably take your abilities for granted. You may never have thought of yourself as part of nondisabled, dominant culture.

At the same time, it is important to note that having a disability does not mean that a person automatically identifies with Disability Culture—a community that has its own norms, language, and beliefs. For example, people who are born or later become deaf or hard of hearing may not identify with Deaf Culture (which is signified by a capital *D*) and has its own language, norms, and beliefs.

R stands for "Religion and spirituality." In the United States, religious minorities include Muslims, Jews, Hindus, and Buddhists, along with a smaller number of people who hold other non-Christian identities (e.g., Shinto, Zorastrian, and Sufi). Although some groups of Christians consider themselves minorities (e.g., fundamentalist Christians, Mormons, Jehovah's Witnesses), the dominant U.S. culture gives particular privileges to those of any Christian heritage over people of non-Christian heritage.

E stands for "Ethnic and racial identity." In the United States, ethnic and racial minorities include people of African, Latino, Asian, Native, South Asian, Pacific Island, Arab, and Middle Eastern ethnicities (along with cultures within these broader groups—e.g., Korean, Japanese, Chinese, Thai, and people of other Asian identities). Middle-Eastern cultures include many non-Arab cultures (e.g., Kurdish, Turkish, and Iranian people).

S stands for "Socioeconomic status," which is commonly defined by income, occupation, and education. Minority groups include people who are living in poverty, often in rural or inner-city areas, where resources are limited and educational opportunities are poor.

The second *S* stands for "Sexual orientation." Minority groups include people who identify as gay, lesbian, or bisexual.

I stands for "Indigenous heritage," which refers to American Indian, Alaska Native, Native Hawaiian, and other Indigenous people. Although in the United States many Native people consider themselves to be members of an *ethnic* minority, this is not the case in all countries. For example, in Canada many Indigenous people refer to themselves as the *First Nations* because they preceded everyone who immigrated to the country. This includes the French and English who came as colonizers and are referred to as the *Second Nations*, and all other ethnic groups who are described as the *Third Nations*. First Nations people encounter prejudice and discrimination as do Third Nations people; however, the former have unique concerns related to land, water, fishing, and other rights. Many Native people identify with the worldwide movement of Indigenous people.

N stands for "National origin." Minority groups include people who were born in another country and often speak English as a second language (e.g., immigrants, refugees, and international students).

G stands for "Gender." Minority groups include women and people who identify as transgender.

When you read this list, you may be thinking of other groups that could be defined as minority cultures and wondering why they are not included in the ADDRESSING list (e.g., the business world, the military, academia, the Alcoholics Anonymous recovery community). The reason for choosing the particular ADDRESSING groups is that they are groups that have experienced a history of systematic, institutionalized oppression—not isolated incidents of prejudice or discrimination. In addition, these groups have been highlighted by several major helping professions (e.g., the American Psychological Association, the American Counseling Association, and the National Association of Social Workers) as requiring special attention due to chronic neglect by the helping professions and the dominant culture.

Consider this: Although this book focuses on nine minority cultures within the United States, the ADDRESSING framework can be used to think about the diversity within any group (e.g., diversity within the U.S. military related to age and generational influences, disability/physical abilities, religion, ethnic and racial identity, and so on). Is there a group not included here that you are thinking of?

One way to begin exploring cultural influences on yourself is to start with the ADDRESSING acronym, using it as a mirror to recognize and reflect on the cultural influences on you. Whether you belong to the dominant cultural group or minority group (or both) in each domain, you have still been influenced. Take a look at the example of Diane in Table 2.2 to gain an idea of the kind of information to be looking for with regard to yourself.

Table 2.2.   Diane's *ADDRESSING* Culture Sketch

Age and generational influences: I am in my 50s; a post–World War II baby boomer; affected by the women's movement, Vietnam War, and hopefulness of college years in Chicago in the 1970s.
Developmental or other Disability: I am 40 pounds overweight, but I don't consider this a disability, although it contributes to my back pain and knee problems. My back pain and knee problems do not keep me from most activities, so I don't consider them disabilities either. I was a caregiver for one year for my dad who was disabled by a stroke before he died.
Religion and spirituality: I grew up Methodist but no longer practice. I occasionally attend a Unitarian church and hold some Buddhist beliefs. Being in nature feels spiritual to me.
Ethnic and racial identity: Mom was French/German and from her I learned French words and how to make pastries, but she minimized the German because of prejudice against Germans after World War II. My father was Scotch/English/Irish. I married into a Puerto Rican family and have two bicultural, bilingual kids.
Socioeconomic status: Dad and Grandpa worked for the railroad, and Mom was a homemaker. I grew up in a rural, working-class town in Illinois. My brother and I were the first in our family to attend college, and I am now an urban, middle-class high school teacher.
Sexual orientation: I am heterosexual, but my brother is gay. Our parents have finally accepted this and his partner.
Indigenous heritage: I do not have any Indigenous heritage that I know of, nor do I know any Native people personally.
National origin: I was born and grew up in the United States; English is my first language, but I speak functional Spanish.
Gender: I had a traditional upbringing regarding women's roles, but the women's movement influenced my values and beliefs. Currently, I am in a female-dominated profession (teacher). My roles as wife and mother are very important to me.

Source: Adapted from Hays, P.A. (2008). *Addressing cultural complexities in practice: Assessment, diagnosis, and therapy.* Washington, DC: American Psychological Association.

Now take a few minutes to answer the following questions regarding each influence on you. There may be some overlap between the areas of influence, so feel free to add information that is not addressed by these questions. Try to approach the exercise with curiosity, letting go of judgments of yourself or what you think you "should have" experienced. There are no right or wrong answers, no right or wrong identities, because every individual is unique. The point is to increase awareness of the influences on your values, decisions, behaviors, and opportunities that you may never have considered. When you finish, you will have outlined your own Culture Sketch.

EXERCISE 2.2

Your Culture Sketch

Age and generational influences: When you were born, what were the social expectations for a person of your identity? Do you identify with a particular generation (e.g., baby boomers, Gen X or Y, second-generation immigrant, etc.)? How have your values and worldview been shaped by the social movements of or influences on your generation (e.g., the Great Depression, World War II, the Vietnam War, the women's movement, Stonewall, Americans with Disabilities Act, the civil rights movement, social media, an economic downturn, political events in another country)?

_____

_____

_____

_____

_____

Developmental or other Disability: Do you identify as someone living with a visible disability or a nonvisible disability (e.g., chronic pain, psychiatric, or learning disability)? If no, has your personal or professional life been affected by others with disabilities (e.g., friend, family member, partner, or coworker with a disability)? How have your abilities or disability affected your life and opportunities?

_____

_____

_____

_____

Religion and spirituality: Were you brought up in a religious or spiritual tradition? Do you identify with a religion or have a spiritual practice now? How were your values and goals shaped by your religious or non-religious upbringing?

_____

_____

_____

_____

Ethnic and racial identity: What do you consider your ethnic or racial identity? If you were adopted, what are the identities of your biological and adoptive parents? How do other people identify you? Are these the same? Are there ethnic or racial differences within your family?

_____

_____

_____

_____

Socioeconomic status: What social class did you grow up in, and what do you consider your socioeconomic status now? When you were in high school, what were the educational and work opportunities available to you?

_____

_____

_____

_____

Sexual orientation: Do you identify as gay, lesbian, bisexual, or heterosexual? If you are heterosexual, do you have a family member or friend who is gay? Is your family accepting of a gay member?

_____

_____

_____

_____

Indigenous heritage: Do you belong to a Native tribe or nation (e.g., Native Hawaiian, First Nations, Alaska Native, or American Indian)? Did you grow

(Continued)

(Continued)

up on or near a reservation or Native community? Do you seek to connect or reconnect with your Native community?

_____

_____

_____

_____

_____

National origin: Are you a U.S. citizen, an international student, or immigrant? Were you born in the United States? Do you (and your parents and grandparents) speak English as a first language? How has your nationality affected your life and opportunities?

_____

_____

_____

_____

Gender: What were and are the gender-related roles and expectations for you in your family of origin and current family, in your work setting, and in relation to your other cultural identities? How have these expectations affected your choices in life?

_____

_____

_____

_____

Now look back over your sketch and see if there is anything that strikes you about it. You may notice that this brief description only touches the surface and, as with the Who Am I? exercise, there are many layers to who you are. I have found it helpful to discuss one's sketch with a partner or in a small group, sharing whatever you feel comfortable with but also listening to the sketches of others. I am often surprised at the identifications that people hold, which are not visibly apparent—one more reminder of the richness of human experience.

3

Creating a New Awareness

What You Didn't Learn in School

Learn from yesterday, live for today, hope for tomorrow. The important thing is not to stop questioning.

—Albert Einstein

Mindfulness begins by simply paying attention. When we pay attention to the world around us, we start to notice things. In the process of noticing, we become more aware of our feelings and behaviors, of the feelings and behaviors of others, and of our environment. We learn information that can help to improve our relationships, our effectiveness at work, and our lives.

Because we spend so much time on automatic pilot, half conscious of what we are seeing, doing, and saying, mindfulness takes effort. It requires observing and listening more, and letting go of our fears regarding the future and our prejudices based in the past. It involves paying attention to the present moment, in a nonjudgmental way. Of course, there are times when we need to make judgments—for example, regarding what we need to do to stay healthy or get along with others. But the point of this kind of judgment is to understand and help, not to embarrass, punish, or look down on someone.

When I first met my coworker Cheryl, I was impressed with her mindful, nonjudgmental manner. She was of European American heritage, had traveled internationally, and was known for her study of ancient spiritual practices, including meditation and yoga. Her studies seemed consistent with her spiritual orientation to life. One day, during a hiring meeting, our work team was trying to decide between a European American man and a woman from a non-European country—both of them well qualified. During the course of our discussion, Cheryl said, "I would prefer to hire the man because he is more like us and will fit in better." Despite explanations of the ways in which greater diversity could benefit our team and our work, she did not change her mind.

I was surprised by Cheryl's perspective because given her experiences and interests, I had assumed that she would see the advantages of diversity. Everyone in our work group of 15 (with one exception) was a White, middle-aged, middle-class American of Christian or secular heritage, and Cheryl's statement indicated that she wanted to keep it that way. Her stance on this issue was a wake-up call to me that the kind of awareness that comes with mindfulness does not automatically include cross-cultural awareness.

❖ MINDFULNESS IS GREAT, BUT DON'T STOP THERE

When crossing cultures, mindfulness requires something extra—what I call *essential knowledge*. This knowledge is invisible to members of the dominant culture, but it exerts a powerful influence on relationships. Without it, awareness is limited, and cross-cultural connections are rarely successful. In my workshops, I boil this knowledge down to six key points.

❖ ESSENTIAL KNOWLEDGE IN SIX KEY POINTS

1. We all have biases.

Cognitive scientists know that human beings are hardwired to put things into categories and to make generalizations based on these categories. We do this to make our lives more manageable, so that we are not reacting to every new object, person, or event with the astonishment and confusion of a 2-year-old. Most of the time this process helps us, but sometimes it does not, for example, when one of our categories becomes too rigid or our generalizations too broad. Let me give you an example.

One day when I was 15 and home alone, two young men in black suits knocked on our door. They told me they were missionaries from the Church of Jesus Christ of Latter-Day Saints (LDS) and wanted to know if I would like to learn about their religion. I had never met anyone who identified as Mormon, and I was interested in world religions, so I invited them in and immediately asked if they would like a cup of coffee. They explained that they did not drink coffee or anything with caffeine in it, but a glass of water would be nice. I gave them water, and we talked for a couple of hours. It was so interesting that I agreed to meet with them again.

When they returned for a second visit, I invited them in and asked them to have a seat, but this time, I did not ask if they wanted a cup of coffee. Based on my previous experience with them, I now had a new category in my head (Mormons) with a generalization connected to it: *Mormons do not drink caffeinated beverages.* I used my new generalization to make the young men comfortable by asking if they would like a glass of water. Over the years, I continued to use this generalization to facilitate my interactions with people who I knew to be Mormon, and it usually worked.

Then one day, I was working with a man I knew was Mormon, and he mentioned something about missing coffee because he had stopped drinking it a couple of weeks before. Now if I had said to him, "Whoa there, Bill, who do you think you're kidding? You can't be Mormon if you drink coffee!" I would have been letting my rigid categories take precedence over his individuality. Fortunately, by then I'd met many Mormons, some of whom did not strictly follow all the LDS guidelines, and I simply accepted that this man could be both Mormon and a coffee drinker.

It is in this way that we continually create categories and generalizations, and adapt old ones to fit new experiences. These categories and generalizations gradually bias us toward particular decisions, choices, and behaviors. Often our biases facilitate our interactions by pointing us toward the most efficient, accurate, and helpful behavior.

Consider this: Have you ever had an experience that contradicted a category or generalization you were holding? Did you change your category or generalization?

But biases can also be harmful. As we age and develop over the years, we may develop *hardening of the categories*—rigid categories and overly broad generalizations, otherwise known as *stereotypes* that limit our thinking and place us and others in a box. Stereotypes can have a positive or negative tint, but either way, they are limiting for both the holder of the stereotype and for the targeted person. *Descriptive* stereotypes describe how a person *is*, while *prescriptive* stereotypes state how or what a person *should* be, feel, think, or prefer.[1] Stereotypes may be totally unsupported by facts, or they may develop from an exaggeration of facts via selective perception and selective forgetting. Either way, stereotypes are used to justify the acceptance or rejection of a group and its members.

One of the most painful ways in which stereotypes harm minority group members is via the internalization of the dominant cultural message that minority cultures are inferior. A clear example of this was shown in the landmark studies conducted in the early 1940s by Kenneth and Mamie Clark and then repeated and filmed by Kiri Davis in 2005. African American children were shown Black and White dolls, and when asked which doll looked like them, most of the children chose the Black doll. When the children were then asked which doll was the nice doll, even in 2005, a majority chose the White doll. When asked why the chosen doll was the nice one, a majority said *"because he's White."* When asked which doll was the bad doll and why, a majority chose the Black doll, and said *"because he's Black."*[2]

2. We are all biased, *but* we don't all belong to dominant cultural groups.

Although we all have biases, some biases carry more weight than others. That is, the biases of dominant groups are more powerful than the biases of minority groups. For example, if you are being discriminated against as the sole person of color in your workplace but your White coworkers and supervisor all disagree with you, chances are high that the dominant White perspective with its particular bias will win.

For example, remember Rhadiya in Chapter 2, how her White supervisor and coworkers seemed to consider *her* the problem? Because Rhadiya was in the minority, there was no one to back her perspective. Even if her supervisor and coworkers were to ask their friends and family members outside the workplace if the situation was handled well, if the friends and family members were culturally

[1]Fiske, S. (1993). Controlling other people: The impact of power on stereotyping. *American Psychologist, 48,* 621–628.

[2]Davis, K. (2005). *A girl like me.* Retrieved from http://video.google.com/videoplay?docid=1091431409617440489#

similar, it is likely they would agree with the supervisor and other White employees.

Of course, bias can go both ways. That is, minority cultures can be biased against the dominant culture. However, the dominant culture's biases against minority groups exert a stronger influence because the dominant culture has more power. For example, although a Mexican woman may hold a stereotype of White men, because she is in the minority, chances are high that her stereotype will be challenged over time by many encounters with White men and by dominant cultural messages that reinforce the positive aspects of White culture and White men. In contrast, without any effort at all, a White man can avoid meeting Mexican women and learning about their experiences directly. And a lack of direct experience with minority group members increases the sticking power of the dominant culture's stereotypes.

In a class I taught years ago, I remember a young White woman asserting that she held no biases or stereotypes regarding African Americans because she had had no contact with African Americans until she visited a southern city as a child where she saw a sign stating *Whites Only* and thought it was referring to laundry. Her naïveté about apartheid in the United States was in itself an example of the power of dominant cultural biases—as a White child, she was insulated from and oblivious to the racism that pervades the lives of African American children.

EXERCISE 3.1

Free Association

Beginning with the first word in this list, read the word and then notice what immediately pops into your mind, noting it in the blank space provided. You may react with a visual image, a descriptive phrase, a thought, or feeling. No one else will see what you write or draw, so be honest and don't simply put what you think is an acceptable response.

1. All-American _____
2. Feminist _____
3. Black _____
4. Muslim _____
5. Lesbian _____
6. Republican_____

7. Indian _____

8. Jew _____

9. Liberal _____

10. Handicapped _____

Because this exercise brings up embarrassing stereotypes, when I do it with a group, I ask participants to write their responses on a separate piece of paper without names. I then collect the list and read them aloud. Although participants are always well-intentioned helping professionals, the associations they make to these words contain many dominant-culture stereotypes and biases. For example, the phrase *All-American* typically conjures up images of a strong, young, White male who has short hair, may be a football player, and so on. The phrase does not elicit images of an American who is Guatemalan, Hindu, or visually impaired—although Guatemalans are also Americans, as are many Hindus and people who have disabilities.

3. When bias is reinforced by powerful groups and social structures, the results are *systems* of privilege and oppression.

One summer when my former husband Jawed and I were working in the desert in his home country in North Africa, we checked into a beachfront hotel for two days of air-conditioned rest. Although the beach was public, the path leading to the beach crossed the hotel grounds and a guarded gate kept non-hotel guests from entering the beach by this more convenient route. The first afternoon as Jawed and I walked through the gate to the beach, the guard said hello and did not ask for any proof of our guest status. However, the next morning when Jawed went down by himself without his room key, the guard refused to let him pass. In a heated exchange, it became apparent that the reason Jawed had been permitted through the day before without proof of his guest status was because he had been with me. My White skin was our privilege pass and because he was not with me, his right to pass was questioned. What was especially painful about this incident was the fact that it was Jawed's "brothers" (i.e., countrymen) who refused to let him through. And this was in a nation where colonialism had ended 30 years before.

When bias is paired with power, *systems* of privilege and oppression develop. These systems—of which colonialism is just one—have a life of their own that extends beyond geographical borders, laws, time, and the good intentions of individuals. People of Asian, Latino, Middle Eastern, Indigenous, and African heritage have biases too, but throughout the world, the biases of European Americans carry a lot more weight, even outside the United States and Europe. This greater influence is due to the disproportionate military, political power, and resources controlled by the United States and Europe.

Similarly within the United States, it is predominately European Americans who have the power to elect government officials and pass laws by majority vote, because they are still a majority. The highest court in the land, the Supreme Court, is predominantly White. A majority of Fortune 500 CEOs, Wall Street managers and bankers, powerful health care administrators, media moguls, and university faculties who train future leaders are White. This dominant group is also predominantly male, middle and upper class, of Christian or secular background, and without disability. In sum, the people who have power are very similar to one another.

Consider this: Think of an organization you belong to (e.g., workplace, college, religious institution). How many of the people in powerful positions (e.g., supervisors, faculty, authority figures) hold minority identities?

These systems of privilege and oppression have been around for so long that they all have names. As a group, I refer to them as the *'isms* and use an equation to illustrate their similarities.

Table 3.1   Bias + Power = 'isms

Racial bias + power = racism, ethnocentrism
National bias + power = imperialism, colonialism
Christian bias + power = anti-Semitism (i.e., one form of Christian bias)
Age bias + power = ageism
Disability bias + power = ableism
Class bias + power = classism
Sexual orientation bias + power = heterosexism
Gender bias + power = sexism

Systems of privilege and oppression affect dominant and minority groups in both negative and positive ways. For minority members, negative effects include prejudice, discrimination, lesser access to resources, and sometimes internalized "isms" that decrease a person's self-esteem. On the positive side, minority group membership may provide a clear sense of identity, belonging, and support. It may also lead to the development of strong coping abilities.

For dominant group members, privileges often go unrecognized by the dominant group because they are taken for granted. These advantages include greater support for one's perspective, interests, and beliefs, along with greater access to information, resources, and opportunities. The downside of privilege for dominant group members is a lack of awareness, understanding, and knowledge of the experiences of minority cultures. This limited perspective is problematic for people who need to understand the experiences of their clients, patients, students, and consumers in order to be effective. Dominant group members may also miss out on learning that could enrich their lives—for example, the experiences and knowledge that come from knowing a second language.

Educator Ruby Payne provides examples of the kinds of information, benefits, and opportunities that middle-class people take for granted in a quiz called *"Could you survive in middle class?"* Here are a few of the questions.[3]

1. If you have children, do you know how to get them into Little League, piano lessons, soccer, etc.?

These activities cost money and are frequented by middle-class people who may be perceived as patronizing by people living in poverty. However, this (as with the following examples) is not the case for all people living in poverty; for example, some people in poverty are not intimidated and may use bartering to obtain piano lessons and other opportunities for their children.

2. Do you have and know how to use life insurance, disability insurance, and 20/80 medical insurance?

Jobs performed by people in poverty do not provide insurance, nor do they pay enough to purchase insurance.

---

[3]These questions are adaptations of a few of the items from Payne's quiz in Payne, R. K. (1996). *A framework for understanding poverty* (3rd ed.). Highlands, TX: Aha! Process.

3. Do you know how to get a good interest rate on a new-car loan?

People in poverty use public transportation, or they trade or buy *used* cars—not new ones.

4. Do you know how to get a library card and feel comfortable using it?

Using a library card assumes a person has the quiet time and space to read, a calendar to track when books are due, reliable transportation to return books on time, and a certain comfort level with the academic atmosphere of libraries.

5. Are you able to repair items in your house when they break, or do you know a repair service to call?

The tools to repair items cost money, are rarely used, and substitutes can be found—for example, a knife used in place of scissors. Also people in poverty *rent* rather than own, so there is rarely the need to repair.

4. Nonprivileged (minority) members are socialized to be aware of the lines separating those who have privilege from those who do not.

I once heard a successful writer (who had dark eyes and long black hair, and identified as American Indian) say that when he flies first class, the flight attendant invariably asks to see his ticket to be sure he is in the right place. The United States no longer has legal segregation, but social norms and attitudes, economics, laws, environmental barriers, and formal and informal networks work to keep minority groups aware of the rules and privileges that separate them from the dominant culture.

Laws permit discrimination against people who identify as gay (e.g., the right to marry and privileges granted to married couples such as shared health benefits, Social Security spousal retirement, survivor benefits, etc.). Social norms and economics keep people who are homeless out of middle-class neighborhoods. Environmental obstacles and social attitudes prevent people with disabilities from accessing opportunities, places, and events. Formal and informal networks prevent people of color and women from moving up in the workplace. And because minority members are more dependent on dominant groups for their survival, minority members have more to lose by pushing on the rules or crossing the lines.

One of the most powerful examples of lines drawn by the dominant culture is in the historical classification of people by race. The concept of race was originally developed by European and American scientists who assumed that people could be classified genetically. Race was defined by a wide variety of criteria, including geographical location, tribal affiliation, language, or physical characteristics (e.g., skin tone, hair, facial features, body type). Underlying these classification schemes were several assumptions: (1) that human cultures can be organized in genetically pure groupings, (2) that this organization involves a superiority-inferiority hierarchy, and (3) that people of European Christian heritage are on top.[4]

Researchers now agree that there are no racially pure groups of human beings, so the idea of grouping people by race makes no sense from a genetic perspective. However, race has acquired a social meaning that needs to be considered from a social perspective. For example, Brazil has 134 categories of blackness, whereas the United States has only a few, depending on who is defining.[5] Because people still classify one another by race and mean something by it, understanding those meanings is important. But it is equally important to remember that a person's race says nothing about intelligence, beliefs, preferences, and so on.

5. Privileged members of these systems are socialized to ignore the lines and differences.

Dominant group members often have difficulty understanding this point. For example, Jane stated that as one of the few White people in an Alaska Native village where she was working as a teacher, she was a target of "racism." But while Jane may have experienced *prejudice* (i.e., negative judgments based on her race), this is not the same as living in a *system* of racism dominated by a more powerful group. Even in this village where Alaska Native people were the numerical majority, Jane was teaching a curriculum developed by *her* European American culture. She spoke and expected the students to speak in *her* (English) language, and the European American educational administration backed her in this expectation. Tests that measured students' achievement were developed by European Americans. And the legal and political institutions of the community were and are those of the

---

[4]Spickard, P. R. (1992). The illogic of racial categories. In M. P. P. Root (Ed.), *Racially mixed people in America* (pp. 12–23). Newbury Park, CA: Sage.

[5]Gates, H. L. Jr. (2011). *Black in Latin America*. New York: New York University Press.

U.S. government. But Jane did not perceive the dominance of her own European American culture because she had never been without it. As I once heard a radio commentator note, privilege is like oxygen; you take it for granted until it is taken away.

Privileged groups do not need to be as aware of all these lines and rules because their jobs and resources are less dependent on minority groups. People in power have more control over their own lives because they, their friends, relatives, and culture dominate the court, banking system, government, college admissions boards, and high-level insurance industry. Because these systems operate according to dominant cultural norms, any exceptions (which require extra effort) become the problem of minority-culture members.

For example, Washington State has a domestic partner law because same-sex marriage is not legal (as of October 2011). Although this law gives gay couples similar rights (e.g., to visit a partner in the hospital when only family members are allowed to visit), gay couples are issued a domestic partner card to prove their status because it is likely they will need to prove it in such situations. But married heterosexual couples, even those with different last names, are never asked to show a card to prove that they are married.

If you belong to a privileged group, it is easier to ignore differences because acknowledging the differences leads to an awareness of unfairness, which is painful. And working to increase fairness involves a lot of extra effort.

6. Privilege separates privileged and nonprivileged people from important information.

Mary took a day off from her busy schedule to attend a workshop on couple counseling by a nationally known presenter. Mary works as a counselor with heterosexual and gay couples, and she herself is in a same-sex marriage. Mary had been looking forward to learning information that would increase her effectiveness with a diversity of clients, but the presenter began by stating "I will be focusing only on normative couples today, not gays or lesbians." He added that there was not enough time to talk about "those people."

Mary told me that later in the workshop, the presenter asked the participants to imagine the shame that couples feel via an exercise that asked them to imagine that "You are a terrorist. You are a pedophile. You are gay." Mary knew several of the participants (gay and straight) and said even the straight therapists in the audience were outraged by the heterosexist assumptions embedded in his statements. During the break, when Mary tried to talk with him about the number of gay couples she and other therapists were seeing, he again dismissed gay couples as too small in number to warrant attention. In his privileged position, he had no need to question his own views, because the dominant culture accepted his views as legitimate; he was and still is in high demand as an expert on couples.

News articles, books, films, television, and radio are disproportionately staffed by members of the dominant culture, which means that the information that exists regarding minority groups is filtered through a dominant cultural lens. If you are a member of a dominant group and do not have any close relationships with minority group members, you will not have the same easy access to minority group information that minority members have. In addition, as in the case of the presenter on couple counseling, if you have a position of power within the dominant culture (which most helping professionals do, relative to their clients), it is unlikely that you will be pushed to consider the perspectives of less privileged people.

Why is this a problem? It is a problem because success in the helping professions requires an understanding of people, and the more you know about a person's beliefs, perspectives, and context, the better your understanding of that person will be. Privilege works against this understanding because it cuts dominant-culture members off from valuable sources of information, often without awareness. And if you don't know what you are missing, you increase your risk of misunderstanding, misjudging, or offending those you are attempting to help.

EXERCISE 3.2

Recognizing Subtle Bias

For one day, pay attention to every judgment you make of anything as good or bad. This includes noting that a program or article is interesting or boring, a food is delicious or yucky, a person is irritating or nice, a place is beautiful or ugly, an idea is important or stupid, an event is fun or a waste of time. Increasing your awareness of judgments can increase your awareness of biases for or against people, places, and things. Ask yourself, "Is my preference influenced by my cultural upbringing or context?"

4

The Invisible Boundary

How Privilege Affects Your Work and Life

To say my fate is not tied to yours is like saying your end of the boat is sinking.

—Hugh Downs

J im is a tall, White man in his early 60s. When Jim was growing up, both of his parents worked hard at full-time jobs, and Jim took his first job at the age of 13. Money was tight, and for many years the family did not have indoor plumbing. Jim did not especially like high school but obtained passing grades, and because he was good at football, he was offered a scholarship to college. He was the first in his family to attend college, and he studied hard and was able to go on to graduate school. After finishing his graduate degree, he obtained work in a field that paid well, although it was very hard work. He took positions in places where the climate was extreme, housing was cramped, and sometimes the household toilet was a bucket. For more than 30 years, he worked many more hours than he was paid and went out of his way to help others. He was able to retire at the age of 54 and now has a wonderful life traveling and doing most of whatever he wants.

It is tempting to say that Jim deserves what he has now because he worked so hard for so long. But such a statement ignores the privileges related to his identity, which gave him the *opportunities* to succeed. Largely because he was a big, White man, he was able to go to college; only men were (and still are) given football scholarships and in those days, preferably White men. After obtaining his degrees, his color and gender helped him obtain employment that paid well, and he was able to take higher-paying positions in places where many women, people of color, gay men, and lesbians would not feel safe. He had no disabilities limiting where he could work or what he could do, nor did he ever need to consider others' prejudices regarding his capabilities. No one ever questioned his right to hold a position of authority or harassed him because of his identity. His hard work was consistently rewarded with advancements and more money.

Fortunately, Jim is quite modest and does not consider his privileges to be an indication that he is better than anyone else. But the ever present danger for people of dominant cultural identities is that they may begin to believe that they are more deserving. When you can walk into a store without people staring or the security person following you around, when you can watch a movie or TV show and the "good guys" look like you, when you can expect that the police will be on your side if you call them, when people assume that you obtained your job because you earned it (not because of your skin color), you may begin to believe that you are entitled to these advantages. Moreover, you may even begin to believe that people who do not hold such privileges do not deserve them.

Often, privileges are so subtly reinforced by society that we are unaware of them. For example, if you do not have a disability, you experience the privileges of walking where you want to go without worrying about the barriers of stairs, curbs, gravel walkways, inaccessible restrooms, heavy doors, and unreachable counters. You do not have to pay extra for a car with special handles, a hotel room that meets your needs, computer technology that you can operate, a wheelchair or walker or other assistive device for mobility, or the services of a person who can help you to read things you cannot see, interpret things you cannot hear, or access things you cannot physically reach. And you do not have to deal with the daily reactions of fear, avoidance, dismissal, and stares regarding your difference.

But imagine for a moment that you are living in a world where everyone uses a wheelchair except you and a few other people. You and other members of your chairless minority group must spend a great deal of time and energy to adapt in this world. When you go to a restaurant with your friends, all of whom use wheelchairs, you must call ahead to be sure there is a chair in which you can sit at the table because all the other customers will have their own wheelchairs. Your neck and back hurt from looking down at people who are always sitting, and bending over to use sinks, drawers, and cabinets at wheelchair level. You frequently hit your head when entering rooms because ceilings are lower. When you travel on airplanes and buses, everyone else rolls on with their wheelchairs and then stares at you as you settle into your special seat in the front.

Although it may be difficult to perceive, if you are of European American or another dominant cultural identity, you experience privileges related to this identity on a daily basis. These privileges are easy to take for granted because they are accepted as the norm. But if you are a member of a minority group, you do not have the privilege of taking even your own identity for granted because the dominant group continually draws attention to it.

I am reminded of a tall, African American social worker in his 50s who lived in a city with relatively few African Americans. During a discussion of the need for health care providers to be aware of how patients see them, even if it is not how they see themselves, he said with fatigue in his voice, "I get so tired of people making assumptions about who I am. When I go on vacation, I just want to be not noticed, to just be one of the crowd."

Randy Roberts Potts (grandson of the late televangelist Oral Roberts) described a similar experience in relation to his sexual orientation: "The best thing about coming out has been to watch myself go from someone terrified of being gay, to someone willing to fight for my right to be openly gay, to finally, just another guy living his life who happens to be gay."[1]

Consider this: If you hold a dominant cultural identity, how often do you think about this part of your identity? If you hold a minority identity, how often do you think about this part of your identity?

Peggy McIntosh is a European American feminist who initially focused her work on raising people's awareness of male privilege. However, as she studied privilege, she began to see how being White, even as a woman, helped her in many ways that she had previously taken for granted.

---

[1]Roberts Potts, R. (2011). Dear Uncle Ronnie. In D. Savage & T. Miller (Ed.), *It gets better: Coming out, overcoming bullying, and creating a life worth living* (pp. 183–184). New York: Dutton/Penguin.

McIntosh came up with a list of 46 privileges that White people often experience—for example, the privilege of shopping at a supermarket that sells foods that fit your cultural traditions; finding a hairdresser's shop where someone knows how to cut your hair; being told about "civilization" and how people of your color made it what it is; being sure that your children's school curriculum will testify to the existence of their race; being able to swear, dress in secondhand clothes, or not answer letters without having people attribute these behaviors to your race; not being asked to speak for your race; and being able to criticize the government without fear of being seen as a cultural outsider.[2] McIntosh called such advantages "the invisible knapsack of privilege" that White people carry around with them all the time, usually without awareness.

Such privileges can lead to feelings of superiority that hinder relationships with those who do not have the same privileges. As McIntosh noted, privilege can also prevent the development of coping abilities that people without privilege use to survive. This negative buffer effect of privilege is one explanation for the high suicide rates among older, White men who have recently lost their spouse.[3]

❖ BUT PRIVILEGE ISN'T BLACK AND WHITE

Definitions of dominant and minority groups (i.e., who has privilege and who does not) depend on the country. For example, in South Korea, North Koreans are considered a minority group, but in Japan and the United States, North *and* South Koreans are considered minority groups. A minority group is not defined by numbers but rather by power. Blacks in South Africa during apartheid made up a majority of the population, but the dominant culture was White. Even when governments change and minority groups gain power, dominant systems of privilege and oppression continue to exert influence, as in the case of formerly colonized nations.

Definitions of minority and dominant groups also depend on context. For example, an older college-educated, Pakistani man living in

---

[2]McIntosh, P. (1998). White privilege and male privilege. In M. L. Andersen & P. Hill Collins (Eds.), *Race, class and gender* (3rd ed., pp. 94–105). Belmont, CA: Wadsworth.

[3]Richman, J. (1999). Psychotherapy with the suicidal elderly: A family-oriented approach. In M. Duffy (Ed.), *Handbook of counseling and psychotherapy with older adults* (pp. 650–661). New York: Wiley.

Toronto may experience privilege in his Pakistani neighborhood but not in the larger Canadian society. An individual may also hold both privileged and unprivileged identities at the same time, as in the case of a biracial woman whose father is White and mother Jamaican. And if one's identity changes, one's privileges change—for example, when a person becomes old enough to be considered an older adult or acquires a disability.

There are also people who appear to belong to the dominant culture but do not, and thus they may or may not experience the associated privileges. In a class I taught several years ago, one of the students made a comment about "our culture" apparently assuming that everyone in the room was European American. He was surprised when a young, blonde woman asked him what culture he was referring to because she was American Indian, born and raised on the Yakima reservation. People who identify as gay, lesbian, transgender, a member of a religious minority culture, or with nonvisible disabilities often experience such assumptions.

For ideas on some of the privileges you may experience without awareness, take a look at Diane's *Constellation of Privileges* in Table 4.1 (the same Diane whose culture sketch was outlined in Chapter 2). Notice the areas in which she has a star to the left of the ADDRESSING influence. These are the areas in which she belongs to the dominant group. For her, this includes all the ADDRESSING areas with the exception of gender. Read through the types of privileges that she lists regarding her life. These may not be the same for you, but they will give you some ideas for exploring your own.

Table 4.1   Diane's Constellation of Privileges

*Age and generational influences: I am a member of the most politically and economically powerful generation in the United States—the baby boomers. I belong to the American Association of Retired Persons (AARP) and receive several benefits. Because of my age (not "too old" or "too young"), people usually assume that I know what I'm talking about and listen to me.

*Developmental or other Disability: I have the privilege of going just about anywhere I want without having to think ahead about whether the place will be accessible and the people hospitable.

*Religion or spirituality: Although I no longer think of myself as a Christian, I benefit from others' assumptions that I am and have never

(Continued)

Table 4.1   (Continued)

experienced prejudice based on my spiritual beliefs. I can count on having vacation during my favorite religious holiday (Christmas). Grocery stores sell the foods I eat. People are not afraid of me because of my religion.
Ethnic and racial identity: As a European American, I am a member of the dominant ethnic culture. This means that many of my values, perspectives, and preferences are supported because they are shared by the dominant group. The business world creates consumer goods and services aimed at people of my culture. I am rarely concerned that I will be disliked, feared, or distrusted because of my skin color.
Socioeconomic status: I belong to the middle class, which has enormous buying power and political power. When I go into a store, no one watches me to make sure I don't steal something. I feel comfortable in most restaurants, hotels, theaters, and shops. Store managers allow me to use their restrooms without question.
Sexual orientation: As a heterosexual, I have the privilege of marrying and receiving and sharing spouse benefits. If I were to divorce, my sexual orientation would not be used against me in a custody dispute. I have never experienced housing or any other type of discrimination based on my sexual orientation. If my partner is hospitalized, I can visit him and talk with his doctors. I have no fear that I could lose my job as a teacher because of my sexual orientation.
Indigenous heritage: I belong to the culture that took possession of the land and water now known as "my" country. I have the privilege of seeing my dominant ethnic group represented in history books, movies, the media, and holidays (Columbus Day) as the most civilized, sophisticated, successful, and deserving.
National origin: I am a member of the strongest military and economic power in the world. I have the privilege of being pretty sure that no other country will invade and take over my country. I can travel almost anywhere, not needing to prove that I will return to my home country or worrying that someone will think I am a terrorist. I have the privilege of fluently speaking the dominant language of my country, and of expecting people in other countries to speak my language. When someone does not understand my English, it is usually seen as their problem, not mine. (I don't think this, but the dominant culture does.)
Gender: I am not a member of the privileged group in this area.
*indicates membership in the dominant group

❖ YOUR PRIVILEGE CONSTELLATION

Now return to your Culture sketch, noticing the areas in which you belong to the dominant group. Using the blank lines below, start with the first influence of Age, and if you are between the ages of 20 and 60 (i.e., an adult but not an older adult), put a star next to Age. Next, go to Developmental or other Disability, and put a star next to this area if you do *not* have a disability. Put a star next to Religion if you are secular, Christian, or have Christian roots. If you are European American, put a star next to Ethnic and racial identity. If you grew up or are currently middle class, put a star next to Socioeconomic status. If you are heterosexual, place a star next to Sexual orientation. If you have no Native heritage, put a star next to Indigenous heritage. If you were born and grew up in the United States, put a star next to National origin. And if you are a man, place a star next to Gender. Remember, everyone's constellation is unique. You may have a star next to every influence, you may have no stars, or you may have two or three.

EXERCISE 4.1

Your Privilege Constellation

Age and generational influences: _____

Developmental or other Disability: _____

Religion or spirituality: _____

Ethnic and racial identity: _____

Socioeconomic status: _____

Sexual orientation: _____

Indigenous heritage: _____

National origin: _____

Gender: _____

*indicates membership in the dominant group

Next, take some time to fill in the privileges you hold in relation to each of the ADDRESSING influences. Watch for feelings of defensiveness and a tendency to explain away your privileges. Most of us are acutely aware of the areas in which we feel oppressed, but we often fail to notice the areas in which we have advantages.

A common reaction when people are attempting to recognize their own privilege is "Yes, but . . ." as in "Yes, I experience privilege related to my race/sexual orientation/etc., but . . ."

- *I'm not racist/sexist/homophobic/etc.*
- *Sometimes I am excluded, too*
- *I am not responsible for what my forbearers/ancestors did*
- *I never use it against anybody*
- *I don't really see color or notice differences*

As human beings, we like to believe that our achievements are attained solely through our own virtue and work. Particularly in the United States, there is a strong belief that the country is fair, which generalizes to the belief that life is fair (e.g., "If you just work hard enough, you will succeed"). It can be painful to recognize that life, even in the United States, is not fair and that you have benefited from the unfairness.

But the purpose of this exercise is not to raise your guilt; rather, it is to increase awareness of the ways in which privilege acts as a filter on your experiences and perceptions. Privilege cuts people off from information about nonprivileged people's experiences, allowing inaccurate beliefs and biases to form, which are then reinforced by other privileged people who hold similar beliefs and biases.

A White man I'll call Lou shared an experience that illustrates this point. Not long after becoming the minister of a culturally diverse church, Lou noticed that there were three, well-dressed, African American women who came late every Sunday, arriving about 10 minutes into his sermon. Week after week, with every late arrival, his irritation grew. He began to believe that their lateness was passive aggressive and directed toward him because he was a White man. When he could no longer contain his irritation, he commented to one of the male church deacons that the women were being disrespectful to him and explained why he thought this. The deacon responded, "Oh, apparently you don't know about them. When they come to church on Sunday, they've worked all night as housekeepers in a downtown hotel. They take the bus home first to clean up and get dressed nicely. They don't even have time to sleep before they get here." Lou said that his irritation was immediately replaced by feelings of appreciation and respect for the three women.

Before Lou learned this information, he had made an assumption based on his experiences as a middle-class White man who had never worked as a housekeeper in a hotel, did not work the night shift, and did not use the bus as his regular mode of transportation. Consequently, it never occurred to him that the women were late because they worked a night shift and took the bus. Adding to his misperception were assumptions about the attitudes of African American women toward White men in positions of power. These latter assumptions were related to his limited experience with African American women. Together, his experiences of privilege biased him toward a view of himself as the wronged party.

EXERCISE 4.2

Privilege Watch

As you go through your day, try watching for the privileges you experience related to your particular identity. This is easier if you are able to observe how someone who does not hold the same privileges is treated.

- If you are a middle-aged adult, notice how people speak to older adults and teenagers.
- If you are a man, watch for differences in the way men interact with young women and how they treat older women.
- If you are heterosexual, think about the implications for your life of being denied the right to marry (e.g., insurance and Social Security benefits, housing options, child custody, visiting your partner in the hospital). Think about how it would feel to experience hostile reactions when you are with your partner (e.g., on vacation requesting a room with one bed, attending a community event in a conservative small town, holding hands with or kissing your partner in public).
- If you have Christian roots, look for the ways in which Christianity is reinforced by the dominant culture (official holidays; in legal proceedings; inscriptions on buildings, monuments, coins; historical and current media perspectives on war and religious conflicts).
- If you are middle class, watch for privileges in your expectations that people will wait on you when you enter a nice restaurant, store, or theater.
- If you do not live with disability, pay attention to the attitudinal, environmental, and logistical obstacles that would prevent access to individuals with disabilities.

As you begin to see the ways in which privilege benefits you, look for ways in which it may limit your understanding or separate you from those who do not have the same privileges. Stay open to the possibility that you may learn something new about someone else or about yourself.

5

But Everyone I Know Agrees With Me

The Influence of Family and Friends

Dime con quién andas, y te diré con quién eres. (Tell me who your friends are, and I'll tell you who you are.)

—Spanish saying

Jen was in her 50s when she met Ruth, a wealthy 82-year-old, White woman. As a practicing musician and professor, Jen was asked to serve on the local symphony board on which Ruth was also a member. Jen and Ruth immediately liked each other and began meeting for occasional lunches to talk about their musical interests. Jen, a woman of American Indian heritage and modest income, was delighted that she and Ruth seemed to cross the age, cultural, and socioeconomic differences between them. Jen noticed that Ruth never called her but guessed that because Jen was younger, Ruth might think that Jen should be the one to call as a sign of respect. Ruth always responded positively to Jen's calls, but after many months of initiating their meetings (and the end of her board service), Jen decided to stop calling and Ruth never called.

Then one day Jen and Ruth ran into each other unexpectedly. Ruth looked at Jen with a smile on her face, gently cupped her hands around

Jen's face, and said, "Oh my dear, I am so happy to see you!" Jen promised to call Ruth again, which she did, and they met for another lunch. They had a nice conversation but just as Jen was finishing her last sip of tea, Ruth said, "You know, my dear, I really prefer to spend time with people of my means."

Later, Jen told me that she felt as though she had been hit in the stomach. Jen wondered, did Ruth think she was after her money? But Jen always paid for her own lunches, and they met in places Jen could afford. Maybe Ruth wanted to go to more expensive places and be with people who could, too. Maybe Ruth found it easier to be with people with whom she could talk about topics that Jen had no connection to—country clubs, private jets, investments, or hiring "good help." Jen never called or heard from Ruth again.

Social psychology research has found that most people prefer individuals they consider similar to themselves. Interracial couples still constitute only about 6% of all married couples, and between 10% and 12% of unmarried couples in the United States. Adoptive parents most commonly choose children who are ethnically similar to themselves. Age-segregated communities are preferred by many retirees. Members of religious communities often prefer to socialize with members of their own religion. And as the example of Ruth and Jen illustrates, segregation by social class is common in the form of gated communities, public and private schools and clubs, and occupational networks and activities.

All these relationships exert influence over people's lives in many ways. Social networks influence a person's beliefs, thoughts, and behaviors. They often determine a person's educational opportunities, occupation, and place of residence. And more subtly, social groups limit or broaden one's understanding of one's self, others, and the world.

I remember the first time I saw a teaching tool called *Exploring Sexual Orientation*. Here are some of the questions:

- What causes heterosexuality?
- 40% of married couples get divorced. [The number has changed since this test was published.] Why is it so difficult for straights to stay in long-term relationships?
- 99% of reported rapists are heterosexual. Why are straights so sexually aggressive?
- The majority of child molesters are heterosexuals. Do you consider it safe to expose children to heterosexual teachers, scout leaders, coaches, etc.?

- Are you offended when a straight person of the other sex "comes on" to you?
- When did you choose your sexual orientation?[1]

I was in my late 20s at the time I read this test and didn't think I had any prejudices regarding people who identify as gay or lesbian. But a lightbulb went off in my head—an *aha!* experience—as I recognized my heterosexual assumptions. With the exception of one couple with whom my family socialized, I had been living in a heterosexual bubble. The dominant cultural messages permeating this bubble-world kept me from seeing, connecting with, and learning from people who identify as LGBT.

EXERCISE 5.1

Your Social Map

Make a list of the five people with whom you have the closest relationships. Whether friends or family members, these are the people you trust the most and with whom you can be yourself. If you don't have five, list as many as you can, and if you have more than five, limit yourself to five.

My 5 Confidantes: A   DD   R   E   S   S   I   N   G

1._____

2._____

3._____

4._____

5._____

Now beginning with Column A, put a check next to the name of each person who is like you with regard to age/generational cohort (see Table 5.1). For example, if you are middle-aged and your first confidante is also middle-aged, put a check next to that person's name under Column A. If your second confidante is in his or her 60s (i.e., a different generation than you), do not put a check next to his or her name under Column A. If a confidante is similar to you with regard to disability, put a check next to that person's name under DD. If the person is similar to you in religious upbringing or current religion, put a check next to the person's name under R. If the person is similar to you in ethnicity or race, put a check next to that person's name under E. Continue with this pattern for the rest of the ADDRESSING influences, for every individual.

---

[1]Rochlin, M. (1977). The heterosexual questionnaire. Retrieved from www.pflagwest chester.org/PrideWorks/2008_Handouts/HeterosexualQuestionnaire.pdf

Table 5.1 Diane's Social Map

Diane's 5 Confidantes:	A	DD	R	E	S	S	I	N	G
1. *Carlos (husband)*	X	X			X	X	X	X	
2. *Anne (best friend)*	X	X	X	X	X	X	X	X	X
3. *Carol (sister)*	X	X	X	X	X	X	X	X	X
4. *Juanita (sister-in-law)*	X	X			X	X	X	X	X
5. *Sue (friend, coworker)*	X	X	X	X	X	X	X	X	X

In Diane's example (Table 5.1), you can see that she differs in religion, ethnicity, and gender from her Catholic, Puerto Rican husband, and in religion and ethnicity from her sister-in-law. However, overall, her five confidantes are mostly similar to her and to one another. This similarity to one's closest social group—also called a reference group—is common because family members are usually culturally similar, and as I mentioned, most people choose friends and partners who are culturally similar.

Why is this important? Remember the sixth key point of the *essential knowledge*? Privilege separates people from important information. If you belong to a privileged group and your closest confidantes belong to the same group, when you have a question, dilemma, or negative experience, how can your confidantes help you to understand the minority group's perspective?

Rather than increasing your understanding, it is more likely that your confidantes will agree with your view and reinforce your feelings of rightness. As the storyteller Elif Shafak notes, "If all the people in our inner circle resemble us, it means we are surrounded by our mirror image." She goes on to describe an old Turkish custom practiced by her grandmother of hanging cloth over mirrors in their house, in keeping with the belief that "It is not healthy for a human being to spend too much time staring at his own reflection."[2]

Although minority group members may also have an inner circle that is culturally similar, at the same time, minority members are continually confronted with the views of the dominant culture because they are in the minority. Minority members also often have greater diversity in their closest social circle because they are surrounded by dominant groups, some of whom become partners and friends.

---

[2]Shafak, E. (2010, October). TED talk [full text of speech]. Retrieved from www.elifshafak.com/ted_eng.asp

At a conference I was attending of women therapists, a discussion question was posed to a group of about 50 American women: "Have things become better for women in the United States during the last decade, or are things worse?" Most of the participants were in their 30s and 40s, and no one appeared over the age of 60 except my mom who was 77 and sitting next to me. The group included many women of color but no older, African American women. As the participants took turns telling about the challenges of working full-time, being a partner and a parent, workplace discrimination, and gender biases in society, the group consensus developed that things have worsened. Participants pointed out that women are judged negatively if they have kids and work outside the home ("You are selfishly placing your career above your children."); judged negatively if they stay home with the kids ("You have no identity beyond wife and mother."); judged negatively if they have no kids ("Why don't you have children?"); judged negatively if they are single ("Something must be wrong with you."); and judged negatively if they are in a relationship with another woman ("You are abnormal.").

My mom did not speak up at the time, but later as we were talking about the discussion, she said emphatically, "Things *have* changed." We agreed that if there had been older, African American women present, the discussion would have been quite different. Even for middle-class, White women, Mom listed many examples of the way things used to be. When she was first married, a woman needed her husband's permission to obtain a checking account. Middle-class White women did not have an identity outside the home, and if they had to work, they were looked down upon for neglecting their home responsibilities. Married women "received an allowance from" their husbands. There was no "welfare" and no shelters for women in abusive relationships, so essentially there were "no outs." Lesbians and women with disabilities were marginalized to the point of being invisible. Women were all dieting because a woman's marriage prospects (which determined her life) were largely based on her body and face. Women never wore pants, and if they did, some people called it cross-dressing. And she concluded, there was no such thing as a conference of professional women because there were not enough of them to have a conference.

But because the women in this group were all younger, they did not know this information, or if they had heard it before, it did not stick because it was not reinforced in their social circles. Because they talked only to other young women, they did not hear alternative perspectives.

If you belong to a dominant group, you may be thinking of minority members with whom you work as sources of learning regarding nonprivileged groups and alternative perspectives. But as illustrated in the example of Rhadiya (the African American, Muslim woman in Chapter 1), minority group members sometimes tire of being seen as multicultural experts and having to teach dominant group members about their cultures.

Particularly if the minority group member is in a subordinate position (e.g., as a client, patient, or student), it may be risky for him or her to share information with you, especially information that pushes on your biases and beliefs. For example, if you are a White, female manager supervising a younger woman of color, even if you and she have a good working relationship, it is unfair to expect her to point out racial, age, or other cultural biases she sees in you, because you have power over her.

The best approach is to educate yourself, which will help you know what, when, and how to ask questions. In addition, to truly learn *from* (not just about) minority group members, peer-level relationships with minority members are a more reliable source than casual acquaintances or people in a subordinate position to you. This means partners, family, friends, and colleagues who can be honest with you and still maintain a caring relationship when you make an assumption that is offensive to them or members of their group. In your current situation, you may not have peer-level relationships with members of minority groups that differ from you. However, as you continue to grow in your multicultural awareness and learning, it is more possible that you will.

Consider this: If you have at least one dominant cultural identity, do you have a peer relationship with someone of a minority culture? What have you learned from this person?

❖ CULTURE SCRIPTS

As you think about the cultural and social influences in your life, you may begin to remember particular messages connected to these influences. Some of these messages are purposefully taught as a way to reinforce family and cultural beliefs, whereas others are communicated in subtle ways. I call these messages *culture scripts*[3] because

---

[3]Inspired by the concept of money scripts—learned beliefs that people hold about money that influence their financial decisions throughout life—from the book *Wired for Wealth* by Brad Klontz, Ted Klontz, and Rick Kahler (2008) listed in the Reference section of this book.

whether conscious or unconscious, they affect people's decisions, choices, and behaviors in social situations, in intimate relationships, and especially in the helping professions where good relationships are crucial to success. The messages will vary depending on a person's family upbringing and particular heritage, but Table 5.2 shows some common examples within the United States, in relation to each of the cultural influences.

Table 5.2   Common Culture Scripts

Age and generational influences:
You can't teach an old dog new tricks.
Children should take care of their parents.
Don't be a burden to your children.
Developmental and other Disabilities:
People with disabilities are less intelligent.
People with disabilities are asexual.
The worst that can happen is to end up disabled and dependent.
Religion:
Never bring up religion in a mixed social setting.
Catholics/Mormons are not true Christians.
Nonbelievers (outside my religion) are dangerous.
Ethnicity and race:
Race doesn't matter.
It's okay to be friends with someone of a different race, as long as you don't marry one.
European cultures have accomplished more than any other culture in history.
Socioeconomic status:
Never discuss money in a social situation.
In the United States, the harder you work, the more successful you'll be.
If you are poor, it is because you have not worked hard enough.

Sexual orientation:
Being gay is not natural.
They should keep their sexuality private like everybody else.
Indigenous heritage:
Native people are slow.
Native people have special rights that are unfair to non-Natives.
National origin:
The United States is the most moral and best country in the world.
Other countries would be better off following the U.S. system of capitalism and democracy.
Gender:
Women should succeed in their careers.
Being a wife and mother is the most important thing for women.
Transgender people are emotionally disturbed/confused/weird.

To understand how these scripts affect behavior, consider one that many White people learn growing up: *Race shouldn't matter; it's best to be "color-blind."* Although it may be well-intentioned, the problem with this message is that in the real world, race *does* matter; racial identity makes a big difference in people's lives. For Whites, the differences are mostly positive and thus taken for granted. But for people of color, the differences are not so positive.

People of color have fewer educational and career opportunities, receive poorer health care, are more likely to live in areas polluted by industrial toxins, are more often victims of violence, and are underrepresented in positions of power in government, business, education, and the professions. Similarly, having a disability or being gay, a religious minority, poor, and so on makes a big difference in the lives of minority group members.

"Color blindness" presented as the belief that race doesn't matter is often positively intended by dominant culture members. In their book *NurtureShock*, authors Po Bronson and Ashley Merryman describe a 2007 study of 17,000 families that found 75% of White parents never or almost never talked about race with their children, whereas the majority of parents of color did. The authors explain how this avoidance of the topic by Whites stems from a belief that discussions of race reinforce divisions.[4] White parents believed they were minimizing racist assumptions by avoiding the topic of race.

But cognitive scientists have long known that from an early age, children create categories to organize their experiences. As children enter school and begin to categorize people by obvious physical differences, they also tend to assume that their own group is the best. So when parents fail to talk about race with their children, their children are more likely to develop racial biases.

EXERCISE 5.2

Recognizing Your Culture Scripts

Now think about some of the messages you received growing up, and list one or two of these messages in relation to each of the ADDRESSING influences and groups below. To help you recognize your culture scripts, it may be helpful to use the following prompts:

- *I would describe them* (older adults, children, people with disabilities, Asian Americans, Muslims, etc.) *as* _____.

- *They are* _____.

- *They prefer to be (or do)* _____.

- *They should/shouldn't* _____.

- *They never/always* _____.

Your culture scripts regarding:

Age, aging, children, and older adults

_____

_____

Disability and people with disabilities

_____

_____

---

[4]Bronson, P., & Merryman, A. (2009). *NutureShock*. New York: Twelve/Hachette Book Group.

Religion and people of religions other than yours

_____

_____

Ethnicity, race, and people of ethnic or racial groups other than yours

_____

_____

Socioeconomic status, including social class, money, and people living in poverty or of the working, middle, or upper class

_____

_____

Sexual orientation and people who identify as gay, lesbian, bisexual, or heterosexual

_____

_____

Indigenous/Native people

_____

_____

Nationality, including beliefs about your country and others' attitudes toward immigrants, beliefs about speaking a second language

_____

_____

Gender, including roles, expectations, and opportunities; attitudes toward women and people who identify as transgender

_____

_____

As you continue to think about your ADDRESSING sketch and identity, watch for the influence of culture scripts on your thoughts about the people you interact with on a daily basis. Think about how these messages may be contributing to your attraction to particular people, media, activities, and topics, and your disinterest in others. Watch for how these messages subtly affect your responses to people you consider different from you. And pay attention to your own internal reactions as your knowledge grows.

6

That's Not What I Mean

Effective, Respectful Communication

*I'm not concerned with your liking or disliking me . . . all I ask is
that you respect me as a human being.*

—Jackie Robinson, the first African
American to play major league baseball

The Yupi'it[1] of Southwest Alaska use the term *yuuyaraq* to
describe a traditional way of life involving three central prin-
ciples. One, everything in life is interconnected. Two, harmony
between the human, animal, and spirit worlds is essential for survival.
And three, harmony is ensured via respectful attitude, speech, and
behavior.[2]

This emphasis on respect makes sense when you know that for
generations the land, water, and animals provided the Yupi'it with all
they needed to survive, as long as the people showed respect by recognizing nature's power and taking only what was needed. Even today

---

[1]*Yupi'it* is the noun meaning "the people," whereas *Yup'iq, Yup'ik,* or *Yupiaq* is
the adjective form, and also signifies the language.

[2]Kawagley, O. (1995). *A Yupiaq worldview: A pathway to ecology and spirit.*
Prospect Heights, IL: Waveland Press.

when a person goes fishing, if he is quiet, slow, and deliberate in his movements to avoid scaring the fish, and if he baits his hook carefully, his chances of catching a fish are greater than if he is loud, throws trash in the river, and carelessly baits his hook. Similarly, respect for fellow human beings works to ensure peaceful relations among people living in close quarters during long dark winters.

Although much has changed in Alaska Native and American Indian cultures, respect continues to be a central value. Lou Matheson describes respect as a quality that Native individuals carry within as easily as their heart or spine, in contrast to the European American view of respect as an honor or privilege that must be earned.[3]

This does not mean that European Americans dismiss the idea of respect. Rather, the priorities are different. African American, Asian, East Indian, Latino, Arab, and other Middle Eastern cultures place a high priority on respect. European American culture places a higher priority on egalitarian interactions that ignore differences between individuals, including differences in status. For this reason, European Americans give less attention to teaching children how to show respect to elders, teachers, parents, and even peers.

Consider this: Did your family emphasize respect growing up? If yes, how were you taught to show respect? If no, was something else emphasized?

The challenging part about being respectful is that different cultures show respect in different ways, and when you consider differences within groups, it becomes even more complicated. A behavior that is respectful in one culture may be considered disrespectful in another. What I have found helpful is starting with some specific cultural knowledge (the more the better) regarding preferred behavior and language and then, when I meet an individual of that culture, I keep this in the back of my mind while I am simultaneously questioning whether the generalization applies. As in my experience with my Mormon coworker who drank coffee, categories and generalizations can be helpful if they move us closer to the other person's experience, but the categories need to be flexible. Here are some culture-specific examples of verbal and nonverbal respect.

---

[3]Matheson, L. (1986). If you are not an Indian, how do you treat an Indian? In H. P. Lefley & P. Pedersen (Eds.), *Cross-cultural training for mental health professionals* (pp. 115–130). Springfield, IL: Charles C Thomas.

❖ NAMES

The most overt form of respect is what you call someone. If you have a name that is difficult for people of other cultures to pronounce or spell, then you already know how annoying it is to continually have to correct others' pronunciation or spelling. If you are the one who has difficulty pronouncing or spelling, you may need to pay special attention to the person's name and write it down so that you remember how to spell and pronounce it correctly.

One mnemonic (a memory strategy) for remembering names is to mentally make an association with the new person's name. The more ridiculous the association, the easier it will be to remember (and obviously you never tell the person your association). For example, there is a well-known researcher I occasionally cite who has the last name Csikszentmihalyi (pronounced *chick-zent-mee-hi*). To help me remember how to pronounce his name, I imagined he was a young man who met a young woman he was crazy about and told his friend, "That *chick sent me high*."

If you meet or know the person whose name you are trying to remember, this strategy is a little easier because there are meaningful associations you can make. For example, I know an Alaskan woman whose last name is Wisniewski (pronounced *wis-new-ski*). I remember that her husband is from *Wis*consin, which is like Alaska in that when there is *new* snow, she might want to *ski*. To help me with the spelling, I add the little saying "Remember *i* before *e* except after *c* . . .," which reminds me that I need to add an "e" after the middle "i" only because Wisconsin is in the middle of the United States. I know this sounds ridiculous, and that is the whole point—the more ridiculous, the easier it is to remember.

Consider this: Think of someone whose name you have a hard time remembering, pronouncing, or spelling. Look it up first to get it right; then try using this strategy. If you can't think of anyone, look in a newspaper, magazine, history book, or online for a name you find difficult to spell or pronounce.

When it comes to titles of address (Mr., Miss, Ms., Mrs., Dr.) my general rule is to use local customs and, when in doubt, ask the person how the individual prefers to be addressed. In many health care and educational settings, there is an assumption that the patient/client/ student will use a title for the provider, although the provider calls the patient/client/student by first name. This use of first names by the provider may be perceived as disrespectful, especially when the provider is White and the patient is a person of color or an elder, so in such cases, it is a good idea to use a title until you are sure it is not disrespectful to use first names. Also keep in mind that although you as a provider or educator may want to cultivate an egalitarian relationship with your young students and clients, it may be a cultural norm and parental preference that the young person use a title to address authorities and anyone who is older.

On a side note, names can be a rich source of information, quickly telling you something about a person's cultural and ethnic heritage or the heritage of the person close to that person. Among many Spanish-speaking people, a person's surname is a hyphenated combination of their father's paternal surname first (i.e., the paternal grandfather's name) and their mother's paternal surname second (i.e., the maternal grandfather's name). For example, the son of Manuel González-García and Margarita Gutiérrez-Hernández would be Ricardo González-Gutiérrez. This custom makes it easier to figure out who is connected to whom.

Along with individual and family variability, there may be geographical and cultural differences related to the same names. For example, when I first began learning Arabic names, I assumed everyone with an Arab name was Arab. But there are many people with Arabic names who are Muslim and not Arab—for example, non-Arab Muslims in Iran, Turkey, and Indonesia (Indonesia being the largest Muslim country in the world). The reason for this is that Arabs were the first Muslims, and Arabic is the language of the Quran. As Arab people migrated to diverse cultures, these cultures converted to Islam, and the people acquired Arabic names.

Arabic Muslim names are usually associated with qualities of God. For example, the name *Abdel-Jawed* consists of *Abdel* meaning "the servant of" and *Jawed* meaning "The Generous" (referring to God). It would be presumptuous for a person with this name to refer to himself without the *Abdel* prefix, because it would sound like the individual is referring to himself as The Generous One. However, in social interactions in the United States, many Muslim people simplify their names for non-Muslims by deleting the *Abdel* prefix.

Other religious identities may also be conveyed via names. A friend recently told me that she was scheduled for a job interview with a man whose last name she recognized as Mennonite. As soon as he met her, it was clear that he had already guessed by her last name that she was Mennonite too. As my friend explained, if you know the region the person is from and the family name, you know if that person is Mennonite. "The Mennonite Game" is a term Mennonites use for the back and forth questioning Mennonites do upon first meeting to pin-point common connections.[4]

Because we are continually making guesses (sometimes uncon-sciously) about where people are from and how they identify, the more you know about the possibilities, the closer your hypotheses will be to what is accurate. As a helping professional, the more accurate your hypotheses are, the fewer questions you will need to ask to obtain rel-evant information, which increases your efficiency. Good working hypotheses also decrease the chance of saying or asking something offensive.

❖ THE NONVERBALS

Silence

In the movie *Smoke Signals*,[5] an angry young man named Victor lives with his mother on the Coeur d'Alene reservation. Victor has painful childhood memories of his father's drinking and pretends not to care that his father left when Victor was a boy. One day Victor's mother receives a phone call from a woman who says that Victor's father has died, and she has his things if someone wants to come to Arizona to pick them up. But Victor and his mother have no money and no car. Then Victor's nerdy, younger cousin Thomas offers his sav-ings on one condition: Victor has to take Thomas with him. Neither of them has been off the reservation, but Victor does not want his first trip to be with Thomas, whose constant talking, upbeat attitude, pigtails, and goofy grin all annoy the "cool" Victor.

As Victor's mother is cooking fry bread in the kitchen, he describes Thomas's offer with an attitude that indicates his disinterest in accept-ing it. Victor's mother responds with a few seconds of silence, then asks Victor if he knows how she learned to make such good fry bread. He replies that he knows she makes it all by herself. She smiles and then goes on to tell him about all the people who have helped in mak-ing her fry bread—her grandmother who taught her how to make it, *her* grandmother who passed down the recipe, and all the people who have eaten it over the years and said "Arlene, there's too much flour" or "Arlene, you should knead your dough more." And she adds "I

---

[4]Laurie Bertsche, personal communication, October 9, 2011.

[5]Film based on Sherman Alexie's (1993) book *The Lone Ranger and Tonto Fistfight in Heaven.*

watch that Julia Child. She's a good cook too but she gets lots of help." Victor responds with a respectful silence. The point is not lost on him, and he eventually accepts (albeit begrudgingly) Thomas's offer.

In contrast to the European American view of silence as an absence of something, many Native people purposefully use silence to show respect and indicate that the listener is thinking about what the speaker has said. I call this form of communication *stop-and-pause,* because the listener waits a second or two after the speaker has finished before speaking.

Stop-and-pause communication contrasts sharply with overlapping speech in which the listener begins speaking before the speaker has finished. In overlapping speech, the two speakers overlap, indicating they are on the same track. For example:

A: I was going to that new store yesterday. You know the one that has the big—

B: Oh yeah, the big sign out front. I saw that yester—

A: Yeah, yeah, that's the one. Well, I saw that guy Bill and—

B: You saw Bill? I haven't seen him in ages, so what was he—

Overlapping speech is common among people of European American, Arab, Jewish, and some Latino cultures, whereas stop-and-pause is common among Alaska Native and American Indian people. There is nothing inherently right or wrong about either form, but because the patterns are learned from childhood and reinforced by the surrounding culture, people are often unaware of their own tendencies and the potential for conflict. When a stop-and-pause person talks with an overlapping person, the stop-and-pauser often interprets the overlapper's interruptions as rude and disrespectful, while the overlapper assumes the stop-and-pauser is mentally slow or hard of hearing.

EXERCISE 6.1

Recognizing Your Communication Preferences

Note which form of communication your family of origin used and which one you are most comfortable with. Then watch for an opportunity to interact with someone of a different communication preference, and try adapting to that person's preference. You may find that this adaptation helps to decrease frustration in your interactions with particular people.

Question and Answer

The simple act of asking a question can suggest that the inquirer is negatively judging a person. For the *It Gets Better* project, entertainer Murray Hill described his painful experiences of being repeatedly asked about his differences:

> As far back as I can remember, I've been judged, teased, picked on, and embarrassed in public for my ambiguous gender. I didn't look or act like the other girls. Growing up, I could never just "be." I was always questioned: Are you a boy or girl? What's with your voice? Why do you wear boy's clothes? Why don't you have a boyfriend? Why do you have a boy's haircut? . . . My body was under constant surveillance.[6]

A related aspect of communication involves the pace of questioning. In healthcare settings where the provider is attempting to gather information quickly, elders and people of Asian and Native heritage may experience repeated questioning as a barrage. People of diverse, ethnic minority cultures may also be sensitive to questions that require disclosure of information that could reflect poorly on the person's family.

Protection of one's family reputation is important for many reasons, including maintenance of the family's standing in the community. In Orthodox Jewish and Arab families, the reputation of even one family member can affect an adult child's marriage prospects—for example, if a close relative has a psychiatric illness or has committed a crime. In addition, historically the dominant culture has used negative information about individual members of minority groups to justify negative stereotypes about entire cultures. For these reasons, as the mother of an African American friend told her daughter, "You don't air your dirty laundry."

Subtle/Indirect Communication

You may also have noticed another form of communication used in the example of Victor—one that is common to Native cultures but not European American. Rather than respond directly to Victor's dislike of Thomas's offer, Arlene told a story that subtly contained her response.

---

[6]Hill, M. (2009). I didn't always wear a tuxedo. In D. Savage & T. Miller (Eds.), *It gets better: Coming out, overcoming bullying, and creating a life worth living* (pp. 201–206). New York: Dutton.

Victor was then free to accept the point (or not) without feeling pinned down.

Similarly, for many Asian people, directly making a point that could conflict with someone else's is considered disrespectful. For example, when an assertive European American states where she wants to go for lunch before a polite Japanese coworker indicates her preference, chances are high that the Japanese coworker will not state her preference. By not stating her preference, the Japanese woman is prioritizing the relationship over her restaurant choice, and from her perspective, the assertive European American behavior is self-centered.

European Americans value personal assertiveness and directness so much that even the term *indirect communication* has a negative connotation. But this form of communication can be positively described as subtle, tactful, and prioritizing harmonious relationships over personal desires. If you are not accustomed to this approach, try this: The next time you want to do something with someone, ask what the person would like to do first, then adapt your response to minimize the differences or conflict.

Physical Touch

Among European Americans, a firm handshake communicates confidence upon meeting someone. If it is especially vigorous, it may be an attempt to dominate. Many Native people have a lighter handshake intended to receive information rather than send a message. Among conservative Muslims and Orthodox Jews, unrelated men and women do not shake hands because they do not touch one another. Similarly, male Buddhist monks do not shake hands with women. When it comes to handshakes, my general rule is to let the other person initiate the handshake and then to be responsive. But this rule applies to me as a woman. If I were a man, I would probably initiate handshakes with other men more often.

In the workplace, touch is a touchy subject. Even a friendly arm around someone's shoulder may be perceived negatively depending on the identities of the receiver and the giver. For example, if the receiver is in a subordinate role or belongs to a minority group and the giver does not, the receiver may feel dominated. Also, people who have been abused or assaulted often have strong reactions to an unrequested touch or hug, and it is estimated that 1 in 6 American women and 1 in 33 men have been the victim of sexual assault.[7]

---

[7]Rape, Abuse, & Incest National Network. Sexual assault statistics. Retrieved from www.rainn.org/stats-test

Among Arab and European people, kissing on one or both sides of the face is as normal a greeting as shaking hands. However, there are culture-specific rules regarding who one greets in this way. For example, in Arab cultures, women kiss women, and men kiss men, but women and men kiss in greeting only when they are related by family or close friendship.

For many Arab Muslims, the public show of romantic affection is considered impolite between a man and woman even if they are married because, as a young Muslim man explained to me, it is suggestive of a relationship that single people would like to have but cannot. On a humorous note, he added, "It is sort of like eating cake in front of someone who can't have sweets."

Physical Space

If you have ever talked with someone whose body space differs from yours, you know how uncomfortable it can be. If you are the one who prefers more distance, you may find yourself backing up, whereas if you are the one being backed away from, you may start to wonder if you have bad breath.

I had one of those *aha!* moments regarding physical space when I was talking with a woman at a workshop, via an interpreter who was signing. The woman was giving me examples of annoying nonverbal behaviors by hearing people and said, "Why do hearing people always move right up into my face? It's as if they think because I can't hear, I can't see either." I quickly checked myself to be sure I was not standing too close to her, but there was a desk between us so that was one mistake I did not have to learn the hard way. A related point is, if you are a hearing person, rather than saying that the person who is Deaf needs an interpreter to talk with you, it is more respectful to say that *you* need the interpreter because you do not know how to sign.

In general, people of Mediterranean roots (e.g., Latino, southern European, and Arab) are comfortable with less physical space between individuals. When I lived in Tunisia (a predominantly Arab Muslim country in North Africa), the women would spend most evenings visiting and drinking tea with one another in the courtyard while sitting on sheep's wool mattresses on the tiled floor. One time I remember noticing that we were all sitting so closely that the shoulder and hip of one of my sisters-in-law was touching me on one side, that of another sister-in-law touched my other side, and a niece's arms draped over my outstretched legs. Although the courtyard was large and there was plenty of space, we always sat close like this—a contrast to my

European American family of origin in which people are affectionate but with much less physical expression.

On the other hand, consider a fascinating study that reminds us to keep those generalizations flexible. Researchers found that, as one might expect, Venezuelans (who have Mediterranean roots) sat closer when speaking in Spanish then did Japanese students speaking in Japanese. However, when both groups spoke English, they sat at distances similar to those of students in the United States.[8] So when it comes to physical space, when you notice something feels off in an interaction, consider the possibility that you are physically too far from or close to the other person for the individual's comfort.

Eye Contact

Although direct and steady eye contact is considered a sign of self-confidence and interest in European American culture, it may be perceived as aggressive, sexually provocative, or disrespectful in Native and Middle Eastern cultures. For example, traditionally oriented Navajo students speaking to professors demonstrate respect via indirect eye contact.[9]

Within cultures, people's eye contact may also vary depending on whether they are speaking or listening. When I was first getting to know an African American coworker, I thought she wasn't listening to me because when I talked, she gave me very little eye contact. However, I soon began noticing that when *she* spoke to *me*, she gave me direct eye contact. Then I paid closer attention and realized that I give more direct eye contact when I am listening and less when I am speaking—i.e., the opposite of my coworker.

Consider this: Do you know your eye contact tendency? If not, watch for it, particularly when you have the sense that someone is not listening to you.

---

[8]Berry, J. W., Poortinga, Y. H., Segall, M. H., & Dasen, P. R. (1992). *Cross-cultural psychology: Research and applications.* New York: Cambridge University Press.

[9]Griffin-Pierce, T. (1997). When I am lonely the mountains call me: The impact of sacred geography on Navajo psychological well-being. *American Indian and Alaskan Native Mental Health Research, 7,* 1–10.

Of course, a particular kind of direct eye contact is hostile and offensive in most cultures. In an article examining her experiences of privilege and oppression as a European American woman, Stacey Prince writes:

> Generally in the world, unless I am with my partner or someone has good "gaydar," [10] I pass as heterosexual (an unearned privilege). My partner Teri, as a more butch woman, experiences "the look" more often than I do—and when we are together . . . and outside of the safety of Seattle, we experience "the look" almost continuously. I have a client who often references the "black tax" (having to work that much harder to succeed and be successful as a professional woman of color) and recently on a trip I recognized how often I experience the "gay tax"—for example, having to prove myself a worthy companion when surrounded by heterosexual couples with whom I am trying to make conversation. I see the look, the recognition, and the subtle standoffishness; by the end of the event a few are laughing and joking with me, and I feel the success of that but also the exhaustion. [11]

Dress

What you wear is also a form of nonverbal communication. I remember a North African man telling me about a time his family invited some Americans over for dinner and they showed up in jeans and T-shirts. The family said nothing about the Americans' attire but considered it rude. From their perspective, a dinner invitation was a special event, and the Americans' dress suggested they were going somewhere unimportant. Similarly, clothes that are revealing can be offensive to people of Middle Eastern cultures.

Because norms regarding dress vary across generations and settings, what works for one may not work for another. For example, although tattoos and piercings are common among younger people and in some workplaces, older people may see them as a sign of immaturity, poor judgment, or so strange that the elder thinks "How could they possibly understand me?" I know of a young counselor who was excellent in working with children, but some parents who were looking for a therapist did not want their child to see her. Although they did

---

[10] A pun on radar, meaning an ability to know who is gay.

[11] Prince, S. (2010, November 30). What's in your knapsack [Web message]? Retrieved from blog http://therapeuticjustice.blogspot.com/2010/11/whats-in-your-knapsack.html

not say it, I suspect their decision was related to distrust and/or concern that their child would be impressed with her tattoos and dress and want the same thing.

If you notice yourself feeling defensive regarding other people's views of your dress, thinking about your priorities may help you figure out what to do (or rather, wear). If the relationship is your priority, then you may want to change what you wear. However, if something else is more important to you (e.g., your sense of self, self-expression, or comfort), changing your attire may feel like too much of a change to make. At the least, understanding that others may interpret your dress differently than you intend can help you avoid misunderstandings.

Miscellaneous

Another form of respect is speaking directly to an individual (vs. talking to someone else about the person when the individual is present). This might seem obvious, but I have seen people ignore a person who is in the room simply because the person is older or has a disability. For example, an Argentinian friend of mine recounted how when she took her mother to the *mother's* doctor appointment, the physician gave all his eye contact to my friend as he talked about her mother's health. The physician knew that the mother had no cognitive deficits, and although his behavior was unintentional, it was clearly disrespectful and hurtful to the mother.

On the flip side, regarding people with disabilities, don't stare, and don't assume that people with disabilities need help. When you first meet a person with a disability, don't immediately tell the individual about the other person you know who has a disability. As Rhoda Olkin notes, this is the "Some of my best friends are . . ." approach, and people with disabilities hear it a lot.[12] However, as you are getting to know the person, letting the individual know that you are a caregiver for or closely related to someone who has a disability can let him or her know you have some understanding.

Similarly, when speaking with older adults, never use a baby voice. I have worked in nursing facilities, and more than once I've heard staff speak to older residents as they would to a 3-year-old, including tone (high-pitched), language ("we" instead of "you" as in *How are we today?*), and volume (loud). This tendency probably comes from the assumption that all older people are cognitively impaired and hard of

---

[12]Olkin, R. (1999). *What psychotherapists should know about disability.* New York: Guilford Press.

hearing. A similar assumption is often made about people who have disabilities. With elders and people who have disabilities, it is best to assume the individual has no cognitive impairment, and then if you find out otherwise, adjust what you are saying to facilitate the communication.

Also, be careful how you interpret others' body language, and think about what you communicate with your own. Some gestures commonly used by Americans are considered obscene in other cultures (e.g., the OK sign in Brazil and the thumbs up gesture in parts of the Middle East). People who have disabilities may use body movements and gestures to communicate in unique ways depending upon their disability. Among the Yupi'it, raising one's eyebrows is a nonverbal way of saying "yes," which can lead to misunderstanding when the Yup'ik person answers "yes" with raised eyebrows to a non-Native person who does not know the gesture's meaning. Also, among Asian people, nodding and saying yes may simply mean "I am listening," not "I agree."

In summary, although you may not always know what someone else considers respectful, combining the preceding information with a respectful attitude will give you many more hypotheses, increasing the likelihood that you will figure it out.

Table 6.1   Eight Dos and Don'ts of Respectful Communication

1. Do learn how to pronounce and spell a person's name.

   Don't shorten or anglicize a person's name unless the individual suggests it (e.g., Don't call Mohammed "Mo").

2. Do adapt your pace of speech to fit the other person's comfort.

   Don't interrupt a person who pauses before speaking.

3. Do use more subtle (indirect) communication with people who value harmony over directness.

   Don't assume that if the other person expresses no preference, it is because the person doesn't have one.

4. Do try placing a higher priority on the relationship than on your personal wants.

   Don't assume that asserting your position or preference will facilitate the relationship.

5. Don't touch the assistive devices or service animals belonging to a person with a disability without the person's permission.

   Do adapt your physical space/distance to fit the other person's comfort.

6. Don't give steady direct eye contact to someone who appears uncomfortable with it.

   Do consider lesser eye contact as a possible sign of respect.

7. Don't assume a person's dress means what you think it means.

   Do recognize how others may interpret your dress.

8. Don't talk loudly to an older adult or to a person with a disability unless you know the person is hard of hearing.

   Do assume that the older adult or person with a disability does not have any cognitive impairments unless you find out otherwise.

EXERCISE 6.2

Practicing the Eight Dos and Don'ts

Pick one of the Eight Dos and Don'ts that is new to you and try practicing it for a week.

7

Say What?
Why Words Matter

❖ ❖ ❖

The word is a force; it is the power you have to express and com-
municate, to think, and thereby to create the events in your life.

—Don Miguel Ruiz,
The Four Agreements

I once saw a U.S. newspaper report on the Chilean presidential elec-
tion of Michelle Bachelet in which the reporter wrote: "Bachelet, 54,
will be only the third woman directly elected president of a Latin
American country."[1] When I read this, what immediately popped in
my head was "*only* the third woman! The United States has not had
even *one*." Describing Batchelet as "only the third woman president"
subtly suggests that Latin American countries are behind the United
States (where this newspaper is being read).

I have seen the same comment made in U.S. papers with regard to
other countries that have had women presidents. In fact, more than 50
women have been elected presidents or prime ministers of countries
that many Americans assume have fewer women's rights than the

---

[1]Gallardo, E. (2006, January 16). Batchelet next Chilean president. *Peninsula
Clarion*, p. A-7.

United States (e.g., Nicaragua, Panamá, Bangladesh, Burundi, the Philippines, Sri Lanka, Dominica, Haiti, Indonesia, Turkey, and India).

Language subtly influences beliefs and perspectives, often without our awareness. This includes the terms people use to identify themselves and one another. For example, if you have never heard a person with a disability refer to a nondisabled person as a TAB, it may not have occurred to you that you and all other nondisabled people are temporarily able-bodied (assuming you live long enough).

Similarly, consider the different tone of words used to describe people over 65. How do or would you feel about being called an elder versus an old man, old woman, senior citizen, or elderly? Many people consider *elder* to be respectful and differ in their reactions to the other terms. If you grew up in poverty, how do you feel about being called poor, low class, or working class? If you are a woman, how do you feel about being called a chick or girl?

Notice I did not ask how, if you grew up in poverty, you would feel about being called trailer trash, or if you are a woman, how you would feel about being called the *B* word. Members of both dominant and minority groups recognize deliberately insulting terms. But the dominant culture commonly uses terms without awareness that minority groups consider offensive.

If you belong to a dominant group and are unsure about a word, phrase, or question, it might seem logical to ask yourself "How would I feel if I were a member of the minority group?" However, using yourself as a gauge will not always yield an accurate answer, because the less you know about a group, the more difficult it will be to know how a member of that group might feel.

Because you care enough to read this book, I am assuming that you do not intentionally use language to hurt others. However, you may be unaware of the negative connotations of some terms and phrases and that they are perceived as microaggressions.

As you read this chapter, please keep the following in mind. The common reaction among dominant group members to this information is to focus on the variability of minority member views and insist that not all minority members see it this way. Yes, it is true, not all minority members are offended by these phrases and terms. However, many are, and if you are a member of the dominant group, knowing this information will help you to avoid unintentionally hurting someone. If you notice feelings of defensiveness arise, try to stay open to these alternative perspectives and the possibility that you might want to change your words and mind. Remember, this is not about your *intention* when using these words; rather, it is about the *perception* and *impact* of these words on people who differ from you.

❖ OFFENSIVE PHRASES

Comment: *"When I look at you, I don't see color. We are all the same race—the human race."*

Perceived message: *"Your color, race, and ethnicity are unimportant. Any differences between us (differences in our occupations, educational levels, social status, or income) are unrelated to color, race, or culture."*

Explanation: In the United States, there is a common belief that success (defined by the dominant culture as high income and social status) is due to hard work. The implication is that anyone who does not have a high income or social status is unsuccessful, and the person's failure is due to laziness. But income and social status are affected by many factors beyond one's control, including cultural influences and identities. The following are profoundly affected by a person's race, ethnicity, social class, and in many cases disability, age, religion, nationality, and gender: .

- Educational opportunities—Approximately 70% of schools are not in compliance with Title IX, the federal equal education opportunity law.[2] The lower quality of schools attended by many people of color and people living in poverty decreases the possibilities for college, and these days it is difficult to earn a middle-class income without a college degree.
- Work possibilities—Even with Affirmative Action, White men hold 95% to 97% of high-level corporate jobs. For every dollar earned by men, women earn 74 cents.[3] Unemployment among Whites in 2011 is 8%, but among African Americans, it is 16%.[4] Have you ever noticed how in the most desirable urban restaurants and stores, the waiters, waitresses, and clerks are thin, young, good-looking, and have straight white teeth?
- Place of residence—A few weeks ago, an Alaska Native woman told me that within the 30 minutes it took her and her husband to drive to an apartment that the landlord had just told her on the phone was available, the apartment became "unavailable."

---

[2]National Organization of Women. (2011). Retrieved from www.now.org/issues/affirm/talking.html

[3]Ibid.

[4]U.S. Bureau of Labor Statistics. (2001). Table A-2. Employment status of the civilian population by race, sex, and age. Retrieved from www.bls.gov/news/release/empsit.t02.htm

Although it is illegal for landlords to discriminate against members of ethnic and other minority groups, 2008 was the third year in a row that the U.S. Department of Housing and Urban Development received more than 10,000 housing discrimination complaints (and keep in mind that only a small portion of violations are ever reported). About 44% of these complaints involved discrimination based on disability and 35% based on race.[5]

- Health care—You have fewer choices and poorer quality choices if you live in a low-income neighborhood or rural area, rely on public transportation that does not go everywhere, or use Medicaid or Medicare, which many doctors do not accept. You are also at greater risk of exposure to illness-causing toxins and injuries related to dangerous work environments and neighborhoods.

- Food—With the industrialization of food sources and monopolies on distribution, many low-income inner-city and rural areas do not have access to healthy foods. Food choices in turn affect health; for example, 16% of American Indian and Alaska Native people (who disproportionately live in low-income urban and rural areas or on reservations with lesser access to fresh healthy foods) have diabetes, in contrast to 8% of European Americans.[6] In addition, American Indian and Alaska Native people often receive poorer quality medical care.

Comment: *"You are a credit to your race/group." "You are an exception to your race/group." "You are not like other [people with disabilities/gays/old people/immigrants]."*

Perceived message: *"The people of your group have so many problems, but you are an exception—you are different, not like the rest of them."*

Explanation: The dominant European American culture generally considers itself superior to other cultures and countries. There is also an unspoken hierarchy *within* the United States in which White, heterosexual, middle- and upper-class, nondisabled, secular and Christian Americans are at the top.

Every culture has its strengths and weaknesses, but the dominant culture perceives minority groups through a negative lens that focuses

---

[5]Department of Housing and Urban Development. (2008). *FAIR HOUSING— PART 2: Interesting statistics* (2008 Annual Report). Retrieved from http://petriestocking.com/blog/2009/07/10/fair-housing-part-2-interesting-statistics-from-huds-2008-annual-report/

[6]National Diabetes Information Clearinghouse. Fast facts on diabetes. Retrieved from http://diabetes.niddk.nih.gov/dm/pubs/statistics

on the negatives and dismisses or overlooks the strengths. But minority cultures have made enormous contributions to the dominant culture in the form of healing practices, inventions, art, survival knowledge, and so on. In addition to ethnic cultures' contributions and strengths, other minority groups have also contributed positively to the dominant culture in ways that go unrecognized. For example, in her humorous book *How the Homosexuals Saved Civilization,* author Cathy Crimmins[7] describes the contributions of gay male culture to modern American music, theater, film, fashion, men's health and body image, and attitudes regarding human sexuality.

Citing research by Gary Gates of the Urban Institute in Washington and Richard Florida of Carnegie Mellon University, Crimmins explains that gay men are risk takers and thus more likely to move into and improve areas with high crime rates, older homes, and rising property values. Cities that have a large gay population are known for their technology and creativity (the top-five, high-tech cities are San Francisco; Washington, DC; Boston; Atlanta; and San Diego). Workplace policies that benefit domestic partners and gay couples, along with the attitudes and environment created by gay-friendly communities, also attract college graduates looking for diverse and tolerant neighborhoods.

Comment: "We need to address the plight of those poor [Haitians, inner-city Blacks, Appalachians, etc.]."

Perceived message: "We, who are better off, know what you need."

Explanation: This is a variation of the negative focus on minority groups but one that is difficult to recognize because it takes the form of concern about an individual or group. I am not talking about a caring attitude and behavior toward people who have fewer material resources; of course, it is good to be kind and generous. But the terms *plight* and *poor* used in this way suggest that the speaker believes he or she is better than those the speaker intends to help. Being better off financially is subtly generalized to being better in all ways—intelligence, responsibility, success, respectability, and so on. People of color may be seen as less competent, people with disabilities as deficient, African American men as criminal, Muslims as dangerous, elders as pitiable, and gay, lesbian, and transgender individuals as abnormal.

---

[7]Crimmins, C. (2004). *How the homosexuals saved civilization.* New York: Penguin.

Comment: *"Asians are good at math."* (Variation: *Blacks are naturally athletic.*)

Perceived message: *"You are all alike."*

Explanation: To a non-Asian person, this may sound like a compliment. But if you happen to be an Asian person who is not good at math, where does this comment leave you? Even a positive stereotype is still a stereotype. The similar statement regarding African Americans involves a stereotype based in the assumption that physical ability is the only ability African Americans have. The problem with stereotypes is that they lock people into expectations that then shape others' attitudes and behaviors.

Stereotypes are especially hard to counter if you have limited experience with a particular group. If you only know one member of the group and that member fits the stereotypical behavior, then that one example reinforces your stereotype. On the other hand, if you have ongoing, in-depth experience with a group, before long you will recognize the within-group diversity and the stereotype will no longer seem valid.

Cross-cultural research has found that when you look at almost any group, there is as much diversity within a group as between groups. Take the example of skin color and racial identity. There are light-skinned African Americans who identify as Black although their skin color is lighter than that of some darker skinned people who identify as White.

When stereotypes are reinforced by a privileged perspective, huge distortions and inconsistencies occur without the dominant group's awareness. For example, the number of Muslims involved in terrorist activities is minuscule compared to the number of peaceful Muslims worldwide. However, because this minuscule number receives so much media attention through the dominant cultural lens and peaceful Muslims receive almost none, the link has been made in many Westerners' minds that Muslims are terrorists and Islam is a violent religion.

But I have never heard anyone suggest that because the Oklahoma City bomber Timothy McVeigh and the White supremacists of northern Idaho were Christian that all Christians are terrorists and Christianity is a violent religion. Because most White Americans have Christian roots, they know many Christian examples that counter any generalization about Christians as terrorists before it becomes a stereotype. However, most non-Muslim Americans do not have a close relationship with even one Muslim person.

Earlier I mentioned that stereotypes can exist in the absence of any facts or they can develop from an exaggeration of facts. Returning to the statement regarding Asian people, one of the explanations I have heard for the origin of this belief is that U.S. immigration policies regarding Asians (e.g., from China, Japan, the Philippines) and South Asians (e.g., India and Pakistan) favor people who have higher education and the income to resettle in the United States without public assistance. Rather than make a blanket statement about Asians, a more accurate, nonstereotyping statement would be something specific such as "East Indians living in the United States have a higher percentage of college graduates and doctoral degrees than the general U.S. population."

In sum, whether or not there is any basis to a stereotype, both positive and negative ones work against the formation of relationships because no one wants to be seen or treated as a generalization.

Additional Phrases

Statement: "I don't have a culture." "I wish I had a culture like you do."

Perceived message: "Your minority culture is such a wonderful thing. It must make you feel special. I don't see why you complain or object." This statement suggests that the speaker is so immersed in the dominant culture that the person cannot see the disadvantages of minority status.

Statement: (To a person of color or someone who speaks English as a second language) "Where are you from?" "Where were you born?"

Perceived message: "You can't be American because your skin is not white enough, you have an accent, you wear the wrong clothes . . ."

Statement: (From member of a dominant group to member of a minority group) "I know what you have been through because I . . ."

Perceived message: "I have experienced oppression that is as hurtful as yours, but I don't complain."

Statement: (To a biracial person) "What are you?"

Perceived message: "I need to know your exact race/ethnicity so that I know how I should or should not behave with you and what I can and cannot say to you."

❖ OFFENSIVE WORDS

- **You people, those people, them, we**—Depending on the context, these terms can connote an *us vs. them* attitude
- **(Illegal) alien**—implies a person is so foreign as to be from a different planet; a better term is *undocumented*
- **Oriental**—used by colonial powers when describing Asia and the Arab world in stereotypical ways; better terms are *Asian, Arab,* or the specific culture/country (e.g., *Chinese, Korean, Moroccan, Egyptian*)
- **Crippled**—implies incapable, pathetic, helpless
- **Invalid**—a combination of the words *in* and *valid* meaning having no validity
- **Deaf and dumb, brain damaged, confined to a wheelchair, wheelchair bound, the mentally ill**—pejorative terms that define a person by disability; prefer *person first* language—for example, "he *uses* a wheelchair," "person living with a psychiatric condition," "disability community," "person *with* a disability" (although some individuals with disabilities use the phrase *disabled person*)[8]
- **Primitive/Third World/underdeveloped/peasants**—implies less intelligent, slow, less advanced, ignorant (For example, the art of people in poorer countries is often called primitive or folk art/music, whereas richer countries describe theirs as high and classical.)
- **Indian giver**—suggests that Native people cannot be trusted because they will take away what they have given you; ironic, given the fact that treaties were primarily violated by Whites
- **Non-White**—suggests White is the standard by which everything else is measured; lumps together everyone who is not seen as White
- **Mulatto**—refers to a person of biracial heritage and comes from the word *mule*, which is the sterile offspring of a horse and a donkey
- **Redskins and other slang for Indian people**—used in sports (Consider that you would never call a team Blackskins.)
- **Black used as a synonym for *bad, sick,* or *evil*** —black market, Black Monday, black sheep, black humor, blackballed

[8]Mona, L. R., Romessner-Scehnet, J. M., Cameron, R. P., & Cardenas, V. (2006). Cognitive-Behavior therapy and people with disabilities. In P. A. Hays & G. Y. Iwamasa (Eds.), *Culturally responsive cognitive-behavioral therapy: Assessment, practice, and supervision* (pp. 199–222). Washington, DC: American Psychological Association.

❖ MEANINGS OF ETHNIC AND RACIAL IDENTIFICATIONS

The term *African American* refers to a culture, and usually *Black* (capitalized) does too. However, sometimes the word *Black* has a negative connotation—for example, when it is used in a way that identifies someone by focusing solely on the person's skin color, as in "the Black man in the group." Contrast this with "the African American man in the group," which is more suggestive of the person's culture than physical appearance. But not all people of African heritage consider themselves African American. People who were born in another country commonly identify themselves by a specific national or geographical origin (e.g., Kenyan, Haitian, Brazilian, Jamaican).

In urban and more northern areas of the United States, many Spanish-speaking people identify as *Latino* (men) or *Latina* (women). However, some Spanish-speaking people do not like this term. As a young man from rural Texas once told me, "Latino makes me sound like I'm in a gang." He preferred the term *Hispanic*. However, Hispanic is disliked by some people because it was invented by the U.S. Census Bureau to lump together people presumed to be of Spanish origin whether they are or not (Central American Indians, Mexican Americans, Cuban Americans, Puerto Ricans, Dominicans, and South Americans of African and Spanish heritage, including Brazilians who speak Portuguese, not Spanish). In New Mexico, many of the descendents of the Spanish colonizers of the U.S. Southwest identify themselves as *Spanish*. And in California, there are people who prefer to identify as *Chicano* (man) or *Chicana* (woman). Many Spanish-speaking people with recent immigration histories prefer to be identified by their country of origin (e.g., Chilean, Peruvian, etc.).

The terms *Native, Indigenous,* and *Aboriginal* all refer to people who originally inhabited any area (i.e., *Aboriginal* used as an adjective does not apply only to Australia). In Australia, the term *Aborigine* is considered offensive, *Aboriginal Australians* is acceptable, and the best is to use the specific culture or clan name. In the continental United States, Indigenous people frequently refer to themselves as American Indian, whereas Indigenous people of Hawaii refer to themselves as Native Hawaiians, and in Alaska as *Alaska Native* (*not* Native Alaskan) or by specific culture. Alaska Native cultures include groups that are Indian (e.g., Athabascan, Tlingit, Haida, Tsimshian) and those that are not Indian (e.g., Yup'ik, Iñupiaq, Cu'pik, Siberian Yup'ik, Aleut/Unangan, and Alutiiq/Sugpiaq). In Canada, some Indigenous Canadians use the term *First Nations,* and some do not because it may be interpreted as leaving out the Métis of mixed Aboriginal and European heritage and the Iñuit of Arctic Canada.

Reclaimed Words: Identifying Oneself

Okay, before you decide you will never speak again, I'm going to share with you one more point about language. There are some words that in-group members use among themselves that outsiders consider offensive and that in-group members would be offended by if outsiders used them.

For example, although the words *queer, butch,* and *dyke* used to be considered slurs by heterosexual *and* gay communities, in recent years, sexual minorities have reclaimed these words and now use them as self-identifications in a positive way. However, as a general rule, it is not okay for straight people to use these terms, although it is acceptable for heterosexuals to use the acronym LGBT and LGBTQ (which stands for lesbian, gay, bisexual, transgender, queer). Similarly, some people with disabilities use the term *crip* or *cripple* to refer to themselves, but it is not okay for people who do not have disabilities to use it. This idea of reclaiming an offensive word is considered a form of empowerment by group members.

Having the right to identify oneself is an important form of empowerment for members of minority groups whose identities have historically been defined by the dominant culture. Sometimes self-identification results in new identities. For example, a growing number of people now identify as *biracial* rather than as one sole racial or ethnic group.

The term *biracial* is not offensive, but it *is* offensive to insist that a person identify according to someone else's expectations. As C. B. Williams[9] explains:

> I . . . have had to respond to accusations—by both Blacks and Whites—of being an impostor regarding the impact of racism in my life. I have been queried about my racial identity (or, erroneously, my "nationality"). People, mostly White, have wondered why I do not choose to "pass" as White. Other people, mostly Black, have demanded to know why I say I am biracial instead of "just admitting" I am Black. I have been scrutinized and found to be "not Black enough" by some, whereas others have deemed me "too into racial issues." People have given me advice on how I should talk, think, act, and feel about myself racially.

---

[9]Williams, C. B. (1999). Claiming a biracial identity: Resisting social constructions of race and culture. *Journal of Counseling & Development, 77,* 32–35.

Williams explains that the idea that a person can self-identify counters the assumption that the dominant culture can define identity for everyone. This assumption dates back to the early 1900s, when "Black blood" was believed to pollute "White blood," and laws were passed stating that one great-grandparent of African heritage defined a person as "Negro."[10]

The dominant culture continues to define minority groups' identities according to dominant cultural norms. For example, a blonde, light-skinned woman who self-identifies as Latina may be called White by those who do not know her ethnic heritage and self-identification. On the other hand, a dark-haired, Spanish-speaking woman from Argentina may self-identify as White but be called Latina by dominant-culture members. People who live with invisible disabilities may be described by nondisabled people as "not truly disabled." In all these cases, identifications imposed by someone else denies the individual his or her experience and reality.

In summary, if the information in this chapter is new to you, you may be feeling a bit overwhelmed by now. It may seem like no matter what you say, you will offend someone. So here are four basic rules to use as a guide:

1. Do not assume an identity for someone else. *Listen* for how the person self-identifies.

2. Do not rely on people or media of your culture to tell you how someone of another culture identifies.

3. Recognize that language regarding identity is continuously changing, so the appropriate terms and phrases may change.

4. Look for insider information (e.g., newsletters, websites, radio, TV programs, films) that is produced by minority group members to educate yourself about appropriate terms.

---

[10]Spickard, P. R. (1992). The illogic of American racial categories. In M. P. P. Root (Ed.), *Racially mixed people in America* (pp. 12–23). Newberry Park, CA: Sage.

EXERCISE 7.1

Developing a New Perspective

1. Find a print or online newspaper that originates in another country or minority culture. If English is your only language, look for an English version of another country's newspaper. As you read the articles, notice differences in the content (e.g., stories you do not see in the mainstream U.S. news) and in the perspective toward information about the United States.

Or:

2. Read a book written by a person who belongs to a minority culture with whom you have little experience. For example, if you are Christian, read a book by a Muslim. If you have never had a disability, read a book by a person who has. If you have no friends who identify as transgender, read a book by someone who is transgender. An alternative is watching a movie, but good luck finding a movie in which the director, actors, and screenplay writer belong to the culture or group being portrayed.

8

Making the Connection

The Four Relationship Vitals

Be the change you wish to see in the world.

—Mahatma Gandhi

During a gathering of coworkers concerned with the war in the Middle East, we were asked to share our thoughts in a talking circle format. I had been working with these individuals for 2 years, and there was one woman whom I found irritating, as I perceived her to be arrogant and insensitive. My coworkers knew that I was at that time married to an Arab Muslim man whom I had met 10 years earlier while living in France. As I began telling them how overwhelmed he and I were feeling with anti-Arab, anti-Muslim news and comments from strangers and nonstrangers, I began to cry. I went to the bathroom to pull myself together and then returned to the group, which was continuing. No one responded to what I had said until later during the break, when the woman came over to me as I was making a cup of tea. She moved close to me and said, "You know, Pam, you probably don't know this about me because I don't tell many people. I am Arab American." I stopped dunking my tea bag and turned toward her. With warmth in her voice, she said, "I know how you and your husband are feeling."

Based on her looks and surname, it had never occurred to me that this woman, whom I had known professionally for 2 years, was Arab American. With her words, something in me melted. I immediately felt an opening toward her that allowed me to see her as a whole human being—a woman who was passionate about her work despite her own pain. I felt grateful to her for reaching out to share with me this information that increased her vulnerability. Although her behaviors did not change (she was still direct, task focused, and brusque), I subsequently felt an openness toward her that increased my feeling of appreciation of and connection to her.

The day-to-day work of initiating, building, and maintaining relationships is not easy, especially when cultural divides are being crossed. At least four qualities are essential, and I call these the *relationship vitals*. The first relationship vital is courage.

❖ COURAGE

After joining the Army and training as an Arabic interpreter, Stephen became more aware of his same-sex attraction. Honesty, integrity, and courage were values the Army emphasized, and as his awareness grew, he felt increasingly conflicted. His fellow soldiers accepted him, and his supervisor gave him a glowing evaluation, but he began feeling as though he was living a lie. He submitted his resignation to his supervisor, and the supervisor turned it down, saying he did not want to lose another good interpreter to *Don't Ask Don't Tell*. Apparently under pressure, the supervisor later reversed his decision, and Stephen was discharged. Fast forward to today; Stephen is now studying at a multicultural university toward the goal of becoming a professor and increasing Americans' understanding of the Middle East.

The most helpful idea I have found regarding courage is a definition: "Courage is fear that has said its prayers." In other words, if you are not afraid, it isn't courage. Stephen served in Iraq and risked his life out of the conviction that he was doing the right thing. He felt fear in his job as an interpreter in a physically dangerous place and then in relation to his work and future. But he kept moving forward. He kept thinking, questioning, and searching for answers, a process that takes courage.

Whether you belong to a minority group, a dominant group, or both, relationship pain will occur. When cultural differences are present, the pain is amplified. To weather the mistakes, hurt feelings, and anger, it helps to focus on where and who you want to be, then go ahead and take the steps to get there even when you are quaking in your boots. In short, keep trying.

Consider this: When was the last time you reached out to someone different from you when it would have been easier not to?

❖ HUMILITY, QUESTIONING MIND, AND COMPASSION

In studying the world's major religions, including Christianity, Judaism, Islam, Buddhism, Confucianism, Taoism, Hinduism, and Indigenous spiritualities, the scholar Huston Smith asked the question, "What makes a person wise?" He found that all these religions agree on the importance of *humility, a questioning mind,* and *compassion.* [1] I consider these the remaining relationship vitals. Humility opens us toward others. Questioning (especially our own assumptions) increases our ability to be accepting rather than judgmental, and relationships flourish when people feel accepted and not judged. Compassion is powerful because compassionate behavior facilitates connection.

Humility

I once worked with a staff of individuals who provided care at a nonprofit organization for people who were homeless and living with alcoholism, drug addiction, and psychiatric conditions. During a workshop, the staff shared their stories, including a young Native Hawaiian father of 10 who talked about his hurt feelings every time someone asked him, "Are they all yours?" If he explained that the kids were from a combination of his and his former wife's first marriages, along with two teens he took in off the street, inquisitors appeared interested and respectful. But when he simply said "Yes, they're all mine," he could feel the negative judgments of him.

Another quiet, middle-aged staff member talked about her pain growing up as the child of a White father and Iñupiaq mother. When

---

[1]Smith, H. (1991). *The world's religions.* New York: HarperCollins. (Note: these are my adaptations of his terms: *humility, veracity,* and *charity.*)

she was in her mother's village, the Native kids teased her cruelly about being White, and when she was in the city, the White kids excluded her because she was Native. She worked with people who were homeless because at one point in her life, she had been homeless and alcoholic. She talked about her frustration with physicians who refused to provide full care to the clients she brought to them because the physicians thought it was pointless. She guessed that they were thinking, "Why help people who won't help themselves?"

As a group, the team shared their challenges in helping people who had often lost hope. As I listened to them talk about their clients with genuine affection and concern, I felt humbled by the respect they had for their clients. This team was doing social justice work in a very personal way, helping people build a better life one small step at a time.

Humility is one of the most essential qualities for working across cultures, and conveniently, cross-cultural work provides an unending number of humbling opportunities. The word *humility* is related to the word *humus*, or *earth*, and humbling experiences bring us down to earth, reminding us of our interconnectedness to one another. The word is also related to the word *humor*, and in my experience, people who are down-to-earth often have a good sense of humor, too.

Consider this: When was the last time you felt humbled by a person or experience? (Note that I did not say humiliated, as this is a completely different experience.)

How does one cultivate humility? I know of two ways. The first involves being around people who see the world differently than you do, staying open to the possibility that you may learn something. When we are around people with different worldviews, the rightness of our own beliefs is inevitably challenged. This is especially true when surrounded by a majority group that has more power.

The second way to cultivate humility is to continually question what we know and how we know it. I call this the questioning mind.

Questioning Mind

A questioning mind begins with curiosity, which creates an opening. This opening is further expanded by critical thinking. As Oliver Wendell Holmes once said, "One's mind, once stretched by a new idea, never regains its original dimensions."

Educator Stephen Brookfield describes critical thinking as a process that goes beyond black and white, either/or answers, and involves at least three steps: (1) identifying and challenging assumptions, our own as well as others', (2) examining cultural and other influences, and (3) imagining and considering diverse possibilities.

The first step of recognizing assumptions is always easier when we are talking about *other* people's assumptions. The difficulty lies in recognizing our own. If we live and work closely with a large number of people who are different from us, the contrast between our beliefs and the majority draws attention to the differences. This is why people in the minority tend to be more aware of the dominant group's views and preferences than vice versa.

To give a simple example, there is a saying in the United States, "The squeaky wheel gets the grease," which is generally taken to mean that if a person speaks up enough about something, he will get what he wants. In contrast, there is an equally common saying in Japan, "The nail that sticks out gets hammered down," which suggests the exact opposite. These sayings reflect values, which are then manifested in behaviors that are reinforced in each culture. In work settings, these behaviors can play out in meetings where White men will speak up and talk a lot more than Japanese participants, particularly Japanese women. This is not denying that there are outspoken Japanese women or reserved White men; however, these patterns are common because they reflect cultural expectations and norms.

Another way to notice an assumption is if you are surprised by something, because if you are surprised, you must have expected something else. Remember the *aha!* experience. I am reminded of a story told by a young White man, Brett, who was working in a social services program with African American and African immigrant children and families. Brett said that one day his coworker, Leo, came to the office dressed in new jeans, a button-down shirt, and nice shoes. Leo was a big, strong, dark-skinned African American man who usually wore old jeans, a T-shirt, and gym shoes. Brett asked Leo, "Are you going to a job interview or something?" to which Leo said, "No, I was at a track meet." Not understanding Leo's response, Brett finally said to Leo, "I don't get it—why do you dress up for a track meet?" Leo said, "Because, if I don't, people might think I'm a gang member." Brett suddenly realized that Leo had to think about people's negative assumptions about him every single day, something Brett had the privilege of not having to think about in this way.

EXERCISE 8.1

Questioning Mind

Think of a person, controversial topic (e.g., gay marriage), event (e.g., building a mosque at the World Trade Center), or issue (e.g., immigration reform) that includes culture, different views, and negative feelings. Ask yourself these questions:

   a. What are the influences on me that have led to my view of this person/situation/event/issue? For example, how have my age, gender, social class, ethnicity, disability status, religious or secular upbringing shaped my beliefs and behaviors?

   b. How do I know that my belief, perspective, or behavior is true, accurate, or the best? Does the information I use to validate my views come from people and sources who are similar to me?

   c. Are there alternative views that could be valid, healthy, or positive?

   d. If I put myself in this other person's shoes, can I understand how he or she came to see the situation in this way, even if I disagree with his or her view?

Compassion

We often think of compassion as a feeling—either you have it or you don't. But compassion involves thoughts, behaviors, and feelings. Moreover, it can be cultivated, and it works to facilitate relationships even when someone does something hurtful or wrong. The following strategies will help you to grow your compassion, even toward people you do not like.

Strategy 1: Common Interest

When you want to feel and act more compassionately toward someone, a first step is to look for something positive that you have in common—a shared interest, activity, or relationship. It is important that this commonality be positive because although focusing on what you both dislike or look down on may create a sense of connection, it will also build negative feelings. Focusing on a positive interest builds a positive connection.

For example, I once worked with a White man who I considered incompetent in his job. The more time I spent around him, the more irritated I became by the fact that he appeared to be bluffing his way through his work. We were part of a team, so I did not have any authority over him. I decided to look for a common interest and began asking him a few questions, listening until I learned of his love for wildlife, an interest that I shared.

After that, whenever I saw a moose on the way to work (living in Alaska), I told him about it. When I spotted a hawk that was rare in our area, I described it to him, and we talked about our bear sightings. Although I cannot remember what he said in return, I do remember the warm feeling we shared whenever we talked about animals and the outdoors. (Someone once said that long after we forget what people say to us, we remember how they made us feel.) After 2 or 3 weeks, my judgmentalism regarding his "incompetence" shifted to a more compassionate view of him as woefully unprepared for his job and striving to maintain his dignity by acting as if he knew.

Strategy 2: Recognize Suffering

The more we know about a person, the easier it is to understand why the person does what he or she does. This second strategy starts with gentle questioning that comes from a place of genuine interest in the other person's experience. Simply asking a person about himself or herself in a nonjudgmental way and listening carefully can create a positive connection.

If it is too difficult to keep the irritation out of your voice, another way is to learn from other sources. Of course, you do not want to ask questions in situations where it might be perceived as gossip. But if you observe a person and listen to the person's responses to others, you can gain a lot of information about that individual. Here are some examples of the kinds of questions you might ask yourself:

- People often repeat behaviors they have grown up with. Could this highly critical person have had a critical, harsh parent? How could these early experiences have created pain for her as a child and now as an adult? Does she appear to be happy with herself?
- People who are negative elicit negative responses from others. Do other people dislike the person? Does he have a life beyond work—friends, family, people who care about him? Does he feel loved?
- What are her goals in life? Does she feel like a success? Do others see her as competent and successful? Is she aware of this?

Considering cultural influences on a person can give added information about how he may see the world and himself, and how he is perceived by others. Consider these questions too:

- What was the person's childhood environment? Did he grow up in a culture and time when attitudes and expectations were different regarding work, roles, and relationships? Did he grow up in a religious household that shaped his views?
- Is the person a member of a minority group by race, ethnicity, nationality, age, disability, or sexual orientation? Is the person in the minority in your organization and how could this be difficult for her? Has she experienced verbal or nonverbal microaggressions (e.g., "*She got the job because she's a minority*") that contribute to her defensiveness?
- Could the person have grown up in poverty or be struggling financially to support extended family members? If she grew up poor, could she feel like she doesn't belong in middle-class or professional circles?
- Immigrants who were successful in their home countries often take jobs considered beneath their previous socioeconomic status. Might the person feel frustrated by high expectations of himself that he is unable to fulfill in his new country?

These kinds of questions represent what is meant by the "questioning mind." They are generally not questions you will ask anyone directly. Rather, they are questions that will help you to keep your mind and heart open to the possibility that this person is a human being who wants to be appreciated, loved, and successful too.

EXERCISE 8.2

Looking for Suffering

Think of someone you feel irritated by or who you dislike. Sit quietly for 5 minutes and use the questions above to think about the ways in which this person has suffered and continues to suffer. If you do not know the person well enough to know this information, you can infer suffering if it helps you feel more compassionate. For example, if you work with a grouchy, middle-aged woman who is overweight, you might infer that she struggles with her weight, that she has health problems related to her weight, and that her feelings are often hurt by people treating her badly.

Strategy 3: The Humor Approach

Sometimes humor can help, even if it is simply a humorous thought we keep to ourselves. This is not the kind of humor that puts someone down but, rather, the kind that helps us be more accepting of and open to the other person.

Laura worked as a nurse in a busy clinic, and an older male doctor was consistently cold toward her. She said that he would come over to the station where she was sitting, stand over her, and note aloud her "stupid mistakes" (his words) in front of other people. She considered different approaches, including talking to him assertively about his behavior, but this was too scary for her. She did not know enough about him to find a common interest and was too intimidated to ask him anything.

Laura tried the looking for suffering strategy but could not learn enough information to know what caused him pain. So she *guessed* that he *might* be deeply unhappy because he was overworked, perhaps he had a family to support, maybe he had a teenager who was in trouble with the law, and a wife who was angry at him. Such hypothesizing helped Laura a little, but what really made the shift was when she hypothesized that the reason she never saw him sitting down was because he had hemorrhoids. Initially, when she thought of this, she laughed out loud, and the more she thought about it, the lighter she felt around him. After that, whenever he said something hurtful to her, she told herself, "I bet his hemorrhoids are acting up again," and created a little feeling of compassion for him inside herself.

Strategy 4: The Reframe

The three preceding strategies are aimed at creating an internal shift that changes your view of the person. But when none of these work, a fourth strategy can help you create a different kind of shift. The reframe strategy draws from the Buddhist principle of viewing obstacles as opportunities for growth. With this strategy, you bring compassionate, gentle questioning to *your* behaviors and emotional responses, increasing your own learning and growth. Here are the kinds of questions that facilitate this approach:

- What can I learn about myself from this situation and from my reactions to this person?
- Is there anything I do or say, including the way I say it, that elicits defensiveness from the other person?
- How am I perceived by this other person, whether true or not? Do other people perceive me similarly?

Table 8.1   Compassion-Building Strategies

1. Common interest

2. Looking for suffering

3. The humor approach

4. The reframe

EXERCISE 8.3

Building Compassion

Think of someone you consider different from you and toward whom you feel irritation, anger, or hostility. To increase your feeling of compassion toward the person, try the first strategy of common interest. If it doesn't work, try the looking for suffering strategy. If that doesn't work, try the humor approach, and if none of these help, use the reframe.

9

Keeping the Connection, Even When the Signal Is Faulty

If you want others to be happy, practice compassion. If you want to be happy, practice compassion.

—The Dalai Lama

My favorite definition of happiness is by the Dalai Lama, the Tibetan spiritual leader of Buddhists around the world. He says that human beings are happiest when we feel understood by and connected to one another. In contrast to Western views of the individual and group as opposites (me vs. we), the Tibetan word for I/me (*nga*) is simply a shorter version of the word for us/we (*ngatso*).[1] Tibetans and Buddhists recognize that personal happiness is inextricably linked to the happiness of others.

Similarly, the Iñupiat of northern Alaska use the word *ahregah* to describe individual wellness that is intimately tied to community

---

[1]Dalai Lama, & Cutler, H. C. (2009). *The art of happiness in a troubled world.* New York: Doubleday.

well-being. *Ahregah* consists of a personal quietness and peace that, when shared with others, is reflected back, creating a reciprocal relationship that harmoniously sustains both the individual and community. *Ahregah* can be lost by one's individual actions (e.g., gossiping, arguing, self-pity), by others' actions, and by events beyond anyone's control (poor weather conditions, a lack of animals or fish that affects survival, poor physical health, death of a loved one, unavoidable relocation).[2]

The well-known psychologist Alfred Adler also believed that most of our ills are due to disconnection from one another. A hallmark of his therapeutic approach was encouraging people to look for ways to contribute to the well-being of others because helping others helps us feel better.[3] Psychological research validates Adler's premise and that of the Tibetans, Buddhists, and Iñupiat: the health of our relationships is integral to our individual well-being.

❖ DEFENSIVENESS AND THE SPIRAL DOWN EFFECT

One of the most common blocks to healthy relationships is defensiveness. Even when two people want a good relationship, if one becomes defensive, the other usually responds with defensiveness. This is especially true in cross-cultural interactions, where individuals carry with them experiences of privilege and oppression. If nothing interrupts the defensive interaction, a *spiral down effect* leads to disconnection, permanently damaging or ending the relationship.

To understand defensiveness, it is important to distinguish between defensive emotions and defensive *behaviors*. Defensive behaviors can be thought of as originating in defensive emotions. The emotion of fear naturally occurs in response to a perceived threat, even if the threat is not physical. The feeling then leads to defensive behaviors of fight (attack), flight, or freeze (withdrawal, avoidance). If the threat is a real physical threat, then defensive behaviors are self-protective and may be necessary. However, in most daily interactions, fear is not related to a physical threat, and fight behaviors are verbal.

Defensive *feelings* are not in themselves a problem. On the contrary, defensive feelings can be helpful when they call attention to a problem

[2]Swan-Reimer, C. (1999). *Counseling the Inupiat Eskimo.* Westport, CT: Greenwood Press.

[3]Adler, A. (1938/2011). *Social interest: A challenge to mankind.* Eastford, CT: Martino Fine Books.

in the interaction, acting as an alarm buzzer warning you that you are about to be disconnected from the other person. If you pay attention to the feeling, you can then take deliberate steps to stay connected.

Defensive *behaviors* are a problem. Verbal attacks, insults, put-downs, and dismissals are all types of verbal defense (and in some cases, offense). In addition, one common defensive behavior that is often not recognized involves repeatedly explaining one's actions to justify one's position. I am not talking about interactions in which people need to explain their perspectives or actions in order to solve a problem or reach an agreement. I am talking about argumentative interactions in which both parties have already explained their positions and remain stuck in a negative repetition of the same positions.

For example, when I work with couples in therapy, it is not uncommon for one partner to repeatedly describe how the other's behavior is hurtful. In response, the other partner repeatedly responds with justifications for that behavior. With every repetition, each person digs in deeper, moving further away from understanding the other, and increasing the disconnection. But if both individuals are strongly committed to preserving the relationship, the downward spiral can often be stopped by a simple validation of the other's experience. If even one person feels heard and understood, the other person usually responds similarly, creating a positive feedback loop that rebuilds the connection.

❖ PREVENTING DISCONNECTION

Sometimes the point you are trying to make is crucial, and it may appear that the only response the other person can hear is a loud, angry one. For example, I once worked with a single mother on public assistance who told me that the only way she could get the emergency room to pay immediate attention to her hurt child was to yell at the front desk person (and her point is well taken). However, in most situations, even when the topic concerns something very important to you, if negative emotions escalate, the other person will not hear your point anyway. The most likely way to ensure that a person understands you is to behave in a way that shows that you want to understand the person.

An African American mental health counselor named Latifah described her experience of the spiral down effect and how she changed her behavior to prevent disconnection. She was talking with a school psychologist (a young White woman) when the psychologist disagreed with her diagnosis of a student, then asked Latifah in a patronizing tone, "Are you licensed?" Latifah said she felt heat rising in her as she responded defensively that she could ethically and legally do her job without licensure, adding, "Don't you know the state code?"

As soon as Latifah heard that the psychologist did not know the state code, Latifah realized that by her own response, she was doing the same thing the psychologist had started—attacking behavior that would elicit more of the same. So Latifah took a deep breath and changed her approach. She explained in a friendly way that state law permits counselors to practice without licensure if they are employed by a mental health agency that provides weekly supervision and that she was in the process of obtaining her license. The psychologist's defensiveness subsided, and they resumed a friendly interaction.

In cross-cultural relationships, defensive fight, flight, or freeze behaviors are often triggered by emotional pain, whether that pain is related to the minority member's experience of oppression or to the dominant member's experience of feeling misunderstood. In the case of the psychologist and Latifah, the psychologist's attacking question started the spiral down and triggered Latifah's initial defensive response. But rather than respond defensively again, Latifah set aside her own pain. She recognized that her defensive feelings were in reaction to previous experiences of White women treating her badly and the psychologist's aggressive question. She chose to respond from a generous and compassionate place inside herself, repairing the interaction and stopping the spiral down.

This raises another important point. To stop the spiral down, *both* people have to want a good connection. One person might want the relationship more than the other, but both have to place at least some value on it. If one person does not care, the other person's repair efforts will fall flat and the interaction will continue to spiral down resulting in disconnection. The psychologist's willingness to stop her attacking indicated she too valued the relationship.

In highly committed relationships, individuals tolerate a greater degree of pain to stay connected. This is why you can say something to your partner that is offensive, but your partner does not end the relationship. In relationships that have a shorter history, less immediate necessity, or less commitment (e.g., teacher/student, doctor/patient, counselor/client, seller/customer), the spiral down can lead one or both to disconnect and walk away.

Like Latifah, most people of minority identities have repeatedly experienced intentional and unintentional microaggressions from members of the dominant culture. For this reason, people of minority identities often show greater tolerance of such hurtful behaviors and willingness to stay with the relationship despite offenses by members of the dominant culture. The greater tolerance by people of minority identities may also reflect fatigue; in the face of daily microaggressions, it is tiring to continually be in "fight" mode. In contrast, dominant-culture members are often unaware of the daily effort it takes to respond and not respond to microaggressions, because they do not perceive the slights experienced by minority members.

For example, when a nurse casually commented on the "smelly fish" being cooked by a Native coworker, the nurse had no idea that her comment was hurtful. She had not intended to offend anyone, but the Native coworker reacted with irritation, which then elicited defensiveness in the nurse. The nurse complained vehemently to another non-Native nurse that the Native woman was overreacting and she was tired of "minorities being so defensive all the time."

The relationship began to spiral down until the two talked. The Native woman explained how salmon is the lifeblood of her culture. The nurse never fully understood the Native woman's explanation, in part because she had no previous experience with Native people. Her privilege limited her awareness of the many ways in which she and the dominant culture had made offensive assumptions and comments about Native people. However, both parties wanted a good working relationship, so the nurse apologized for her comment (despite her lack of understanding) and the relationship improved.

❖ FIVE IN-THE-MOMENT STRATEGIES FOR STAYING CONNECTED

Strategy 1: Know your push-buttons.

We all have buttons that can be pushed, and the best way to avoid reacting out of emotion is to know your buttons in advance. Common push-buttons include politics, religion, race, social class, sexual orientation, nationality, and anything else having to do with your personal and cultural identity or that of someone you love. Recognizing a push-button does not mean your position is right or wrong; it simply signals a topic to which you have a strong emotional reaction that could override a thoughtful response and lead to disconnection.

For example, if you have a strong political position—liberal or conservative—and voted for a president of the same politics, the question, "Why did you vote for him/her?" by a questioner of different politics could be a push-button for you. A push-button response would be one that is dominated by emotion, sucking you into an argument about which candidate or whose politics are better and distancing you from the questioner. A thoughtful response would be one that explains why you voted for the candidate without putting down the other person's choice, even if the person wants to argue or convince you of the individual's rightness. If you have a relationship with the questioner that you want to keep, this thoughtful response is more likely to prevent a defensive spiral down.

Consider this: What are your push-buttons?

Strategy 2: Breathe and pay attention to your body.

Everyone knows the advice to stop and take a deep breath before responding out of anger, fear, or frustration. This is good advice and paying attention to your body as you take the deep breath increases the power of this strategy.

The Vietnamese monk Thich Nhat Hanh says that when we are hurt or someone hurts us, a knot is tied inside of us. If we quickly pay attention to the knot, it will usually loosen. But in our day-to-day busyness, if we choose to ignore the knot and go on with our activities, the longer we ignore the knot, the tighter it will become.

Think of this knot as the physical response you have when you feel defensive. Where do you experience the knot? Common places are in one's chest, shoulders, head, jaw, stomach, and intestines, and some people feel it in more than one place.

Because the body often experiences things before conscious awareness occurs, it provides cues (in the form of physical sensations) that something is going wrong in the relationship. You can use these cues to catch defensive reactions quickly and avoid reacting defensively.

On the next page is an exercise that will help you pay attention to your body's cues. It is not a relaxation exercise. You will need to read the whole exercise first before trying it.

Strategy 3: Stop defensive behaviors.

Remember what happens when you are playing tug-of-war? The harder one side pulls, the harder the other side pulls back. But if one side suddenly lets go, the other side falls down. Defensive behaviors are similar. If one person stops behaving defensively, the other person usually stops too, because there is nothing to pull or push against.

EXERCISE 9.1

Paying Attention

Sit in a comfortable position (if you are in a chair, with both feet grounded on the floor), hands resting in your lap, with posture that allows you to breathe easily. Close your eyes and take three deep breaths, paying attention to the feeling of the air moving in through your nostrils and the air moving out through your nostrils.

Now with your eyes closed, think of an interaction in which you felt defensive, hurt, or irritated by someone. Once you have a clear mental picture of the interaction, pay attention to the part of your body where you feel tension, discomfort, or pain. Walk your mental awareness around this area, beginning with the top of the area on the front side of the area. Then move your mental awareness to the right side of the area, then to the lower front part of the area, then to the left side, and back up to the top of the area. Now imagine looking three dimensionally from the front to the back of the area. Notice anything there is to notice. The area may have a different color, temperature, texture, feeling, or vibration, or there may be nothing different at all.

The point of this exercise is simply to pay attention. When you have thoroughly paid attention to the body area, return your attention to your breath. Take a deep breath, again noticing the feeling of the air moving in through your nostrils and the air moving out through your nostrils, then slowly open your eyes.

- What was this exercise like for you?
- Did you notice anything different, or not, in the area where you hold pain or tension?
- Do you feel any differently than you did before the exercise?

Many people report feeling more relaxed after this exercise, despite knowing that it is not intended as relaxation. Thich Nhat Hanh says that this is because paying attention to our pain is transformative in itself. Paying attention causes something to shift in us, a mindful sort of stepping back from the pain and looking at it, which can help defuse it.

As you practice this exercise, you will find that you can use it in the moment you begin feeling defensive, even without closing your eyes, to slow down your emotional reaction.

To stop defensive behaviors, you first need to know what yours are. The obvious ones are verbal insults, put downs, yelling, dismissive comments, ignoring the person, and physically walking away. Here are some additional ones that are common but not always recognized by the person engaging in them:

- Sighing loudly
- Talking louder
- A sarcastic tone
- Rolling your eyes
- Cool withdrawal (e.g., "Whatever," said with a sigh, sarcastic tone, or look of disgust)
- Repeating your same position over and over
- Laying blame
- Interrupting
- Bringing up the person's past mistakes or offenses

Consider this: Do you engage in any of these or other defensive behaviors? If you don't know, ask your partner, a family member, or close friend.

Self-talk can be an enormous help in stopping defensive behaviors, because what we say to ourselves affects how we feel and what we do. Self-talk that feeds defensive behaviors sounds like this: *She doesn't have a clue. This guy is a jerk. He doesn't care one bit what I think. She only wants what she wants. He just doesn't get it. I've had it.*

If you think and say these kinds of things to yourself as you are involved in a disagreement, you are more likely to engage in defensive behaviors. However, if you change your thinking to more compassionate thoughts, you can slow down and stop the defensive behaviors before engaging in them. This helpful self-talk moves you out of your own self-centered space and into the other person's experience. Examples include the following: *She seems really hurt/guilty/frustrated about this. He is feeling angry, and people only get angry about things or people they care about; if they don't care, they simply don't care, so clearly he cares about this. Maybe she had a really hard day—someone died, her partner left, her kid is sick again, or she is exhausted. Maybe he isn't feeling well.*

Strategy 4: Validate.

One of the simplest and quickest ways to stop a downward spiraling interaction is to validate the other person's feelings and viewpoint.

Validation has two parts. The first is repeating back to the person what the person is saying to you, to communicate you have heard the person and that you understand how the individual is feeling. Repeating verbatim what the person has said is the simplest way to do this (e.g., *I hear you saying that you feel hurt because I didn't tell you I would be gone on Monday or Tuesday*). However, sometimes the other person will perceive a simple repetition as not truly understanding the person. A better approach is to paraphrase using your own words; then ask the person if that is what he or she said (e.g., *It sounds like I hurt your feelings when I didn't tell you I wouldn't be here for two days. Is that what you're saying? Is that how you are feeling?*).

The second part of validation involves acceptance of the person's viewpoint and feelings. Acceptance is not the same as agreeing. Acceptance means that you accept that this is how the person sees the situation and that this is how the person feels. It also means that you accept the individual as a person, despite your different views and feelings.

One mental strategy to increase acceptance of the person is to think of the problem or obstacle you are facing as sitting in the physical space between the two of you. That is, the problem is not in either of you; it is separate from each of you. The visual image is one of you and the person aligned as you try to fix this problem or conflict together.

Strategy 5: Question your need for matching views.

Buddhists use the term *attachment* to describe the emotional and behavioral experience of being stuck in a defensive interaction. When you find yourself feeling stuck, it can be helpful to ask yourself these questions:

- What am I so attached to in this interaction? What would I lose if I let go?
- Why is it so important that this person agree with me, affirm my point, or acknowledge my pain?
- Which is more important—that the person see it my way or that we keep a good connection?

In the heat of a disagreement or conflict, it can be helpful to acknowledge, at least within yourself, that you do not truly understand the other person. If you are a member of a privileged group and you have limited experiences with people of the person's identity, it is possible that you cannot understand where the person is coming from until you know more about the person's culture and experience.

Acknowledging your need for additional experience or information to the other person can also help to defuse the tension, because it shows that you value the person's perspective as much as your own.

For example, sensing defensiveness from a young, gay, recently immigrated Filipino man who sought help for panic attacks, the European American, heterosexual counselor talked with him about her limitations. She said she would be happy to work with him, but she had limited experience with gay men and had not worked with people from the Philippines before. She let him know that if he preferred to see someone with more experience relevant to his experience, she would understand and facilitate a referral. In sum, she put his needs above her desire to work with him.

Another strategy to help you let go of the need for matching views is to imagine that the other person is your favorite aunt (or any older relative you love who has vastly different views from yours). Try to transfer the way you think about that person to the person in front of you. Along these lines, I like to think of family holiday gatherings as early training for getting along with diverse people. Even if your family is ethnically and religiously similar, there are usually political and generational differences in a family that can lead to major arguments. In healthy families, people learn to accept one another despite the differences, at least during the holidays.

❖ RESPONDING TO STEREOTYPES

Comments that stereotype invariably elicit defensiveness. If you are the listener, responding to such comments can be difficult because the response may sound judgmental, which elicits defensiveness from the stereotyper, fueling a downward spiral. But there are ways to respond that can keep the connection with the person and at the same time counter the stereotype. Here are a few suggestions. Keep in mind that nonverbals such as tone of voice and eye movements can either facilitate a positive response or undermine it.

1. Tactfully point out information that does not support the stereotype.[4]

Stereotype: *Old people are so negative and set in their ways.*

---

[4]Italics are mine but numbered suggestions are from Goldstein, S. (2000). *Cross-cultural explorations: Activities in culture and psychology* (p. 317). Needham Heights, MA: Allyn & Bacon.

Response: *If you think about it, many older people have to adjust to changes that are greater than those of any other age group. For example, an older person may lose everything in the space of a few months because she breaks a hip or has some other medical problem. She may lose her home, her car, her cherished dog or cat, her social and religious community, the ability to cook and eat food she likes, and her independence simply because the medical problem requires that she move to an assisted living place. (This series of losses has been called a cascade effect.)*

2. Indicate when conclusions are based on limited experience.

Stereotype: *People with disabilities are so demanding.*

Response: *People with disabilities have to cope with subtle barriers all day long that people without disabilities don't even think about. Have you ever noticed how many public environments for people with disabilities are segregated? Why don't all entrances have ramps? Why don't all concerts and plays have sign language interpreters? Nondisabled people can walk up a ramp as easily as stairs. And why don't all restrooms have stalls that are big enough and sinks, mirrors, toilets, towel holders, and soap that are usable by anyone? If you have met one or two people with disabilities who are demanding, chances are you remember them because we tend to remember when people are upset.*

3. Explain that individuals who are more visible may not be typical.

Stereotype: *Why do gays have to talk about sex all the time?*

Response: *The people you hear talking about sex are only the few who are talking about it, and the reason those few are talking about it is usually to increase people's awareness of discrimination. Also, there are lots of people who you don't even know are gay.*

4. Point out alternative explanations for the behavior.

Stereotype: *It is so rude how they speak Spanish in front of you, so you don't understand them.*

Response: *Most European American people don't speak Spanish, and if the people you are talking about don't speak English fluently, it makes sense they would prefer to speak their first language. Even if the person speaks English fluently, it takes more effort to speak English as a second language.*

5. Note differences within groups and similarities across groups.

Stereotype: *Indians are naturally alcoholic.*

Response: *Alcohol is not and has never been a Native tradition. There is a huge sobriety movement in Native cultures. For example, in Alaska, there are many villages (accessible by boat or plane only) that have outlawed alcohol from being imported, bought, or sold. Alcoholism and fetal alcohol syndrome are big problems among non-Native people too, especially in northern regions.*

6. Be a cultural interpreter.

Stereotype: *Arab people are so pushy; they're practically in your face when they talk to you.*

Response: *Different cultures have different norms about body space. Have you ever noticed how White people vary in their comfort levels with different amounts of body space? Cultures differ like that too.*

EXERCISE 9.2

Keeping the Connection

The five in-the-moment strategies are most effective when used altogether. However, depending on the level of defensiveness, you may not need all of them. The next time you notice defensiveness in an interaction with someone, whether it is coming from you or the other person, try each of these strategies in order until one of them works. If the defensive interaction involves stereotyping, try also using one of the nondefensive verbal responses to stereotypes.

Strategy 1: Know your push-buttons.

Strategy 2: Breathe and pay attention to your body.

Strategy 3: Stop defensive behaviors.

Strategy 4: Validate.

Strategy 5: Question your need for matching views.

10

When the Golden Rule Isn't Working

Respectful Conflict Resolution

If we have no peace, it is because we have forgotten that we belong to each other.

—Mother Teresa

Most of us grew up learning the Golden Rule: Do unto others as you would have them do unto you. This works fine when people have the same hopes and desires, but as our lives become more complex, people's expectations do too. Sometimes the differences can be as basic as values.

Because values reflect what people hold most dear, value conflicts can be the most difficult to resolve. However, there are ways to think about such conflicts that can help. Let's start with an exercise designed to get you thinking in this way. To get the most out of this exercise, follow the instructions carefully, and do not skip ahead.

When I do this exercise with groups, I usually hear groans as people feel forced to narrow in on what is most important to them. There are always one or two individuals who refuse to specify their three priority values because it is too difficult. But the point of this exercise

EXERCISE 10.1[1]

Recognizing Your Values

Step 1. Read the following list of values and circle your top 10. If you value something that is not on the list, you can add it next to the "Other" category, but make your total 10. Do not read any further until you have done this step.

1. Physical health
2. Spirituality/faith
3. Love
4. Sex
5. Financial success
6. Work success
7. Fame
8. Animals/pets
9. Nature/environment/ outdoors
10. Family
11. Friends
12. Integrity
13. Fun/humor and laughter
14. My partner
15. Intellectual stimulation/ learning

16. Justice
17. Contributing to others
18. Power
19. Community
20. Mental health
21. Simplicity
22. Safety
23. Creativity/self-expression
24. Freedom
25. Personal independence
26. Courage
27. Balance
28. Kindness
29. Art/music
30. Other _____

Step 2. Now imagine that you must give up three of these values. Cross out three. You now have 7 values left.

Step 3. Now imagine that you must give up four more. Cross out four. You now have 3 values left.

---

[1]Based on the exercise Learning to Grow Old, originally published in Pedersen, P. B. (1997). *Culture-centered counseling interventions: Striving for accuracy.* Thousand Oaks, CA: Sage.

is not to force you to give up important values. Rather, it is to show how *prioritization* of values works.

Most people value most of the items on this list. However, through the course of our lives, we make priorities. Sometimes our priorities are deliberate choices, but often they are the result of external forces and not consciously made. For example, if you live in a war-torn country, safety and freedom would be top priorities. However, if you live in a safe community in a stable, democratic country, you may take safety and freedom for granted and prioritize some other value.

Value priorities also change over time. For example, as individuals age or acquire a disability, physical health often becomes a higher priority. Priorities change within cultures too. For example, in the early 1900s, the exclusion of women and people of color from government and the professions was an accepted norm. But today, most Americans place a high value on equal rights for everyone.

Because values are embedded in everything we do, they play a central but unspoken role in our work as helping professionals. Many of the values held by educators, social service, and health care providers are the same ones supported by the dominant culture—for example, personal independence, verbal abilities, insight, openness to change, and logical thinking. Assertiveness is so highly valued that workshops are devoted to teaching it as an essential communication skill.

In contrast, the subtle communication skills described earlier (e.g., the use of silence, storytelling to make a point, nonverbal respect skills) are less supported. Similarly, emotional expressiveness and self-disclosure are interpreted by providers and educators as a measure of self-confidence. But many Asian people consider emotional *restraint* a sign of maturity and self-control. Many Arab and Orthodox Jewish people would be reluctant to self-disclose personal family information to a stranger (i.e., in an initial meeting with a provider), because protecting the family's reputation is given greater importance than presenting one's individual perspective. And among gay, lesbian, and transgender people, reluctance to self-disclose may represent realistic caution about the safety of sharing such personal information.

Consider this: Are your top three value priorities shared by the dominant culture? By your culture? By your family? By your peers? Are they supported in your workplace?

❖ WHEN PRIORITIES DIFFER

Dr. Lawrence was a leader in the Episcopal Church—an African American man who fought for the ordination of women and the end of apartheid in South Africa. In his eulogy, Dr. Lawrence's ability to connect across divides was explained by his son:

> He commanded respect without ever asking for it. In high school, my rowdiest friends—the guys who stole hubcaps and crashed parties—were perfect gentlemen in my father's presence. They'd stand and say, "Yes, sir, Dr. Lawrence," and answer his many questions about school and home and where their parents and grandparents were from. It was much later that I realized Dad's secret. He gained respect by giving it. He talked and listened to the fourth-grade kid in Spring Valley who shined shoes the same way he talked and listened to a bishop or college president. He was seriously interested in who you were and what you had to say.[2]

❖ THE RESPECT STRATEGIES

When it comes to conflict resolution, respect is a good place to start. Respectful conflict resolution involves both attitude and behavior. Seven strategies for resolving conflicts via one's thinking and behavior are summarized by the acronym RESPECT.

Table 10.1   The RESPECT Strategies

Recognize a shared or similar value.

Expression of the same value may differ, so think about this.

Step back from assumptions about value priorities and what is right.

Power—Consider differences of power and privilege.

Empathize—look for compassionate, nonjudgmental explanations.

Culture—Consider its influence on behavior, views, and beliefs—your own and others'.

Think differently—Use language to positively reframe others' value priorities.

---

[2]Lawrence-Lightfoot, S. (2000). *Respect*. Cambridge, MA: Perseus Books.

Recognize a Shared or Similar Value

John and Evelyn came to see a counselor for help in resolving conflicts over family relationships. John and Evelyn were comfortably middle-class, both of European American heritage. However, Evelyn had grown up in a middle-class, urban New England family, and John was raised by a single mother on public assistance, in rural generational poverty. According to John, Evelyn did not value family as much as he did, because she did not want any family staying with them on a regular basis, and she became angry whenever he gave his mother or siblings money. Evelyn countered that John valued his family more than he valued her.

The counselor began by helping Evelyn and John see their common ground. Although there were conflicts in their views, they both agreed that family was important. They also both wanted to be able to talk about family and resolve differences with good feelings between them.

Expression of the Same Value
May Differ, So Think About This

As they talked about what it means to value one's family, it became apparent that different cultural norms were influencing their expression of this value. In Evelyn's independent and individualistic family, the best way to ensure good relations was for everyone to have plenty of space. During holidays, Evelyn's family rented hotel rooms, which, from their perspectives, allowed everyone to spend quality time together at the couple's house and still have privacy. In John's family, hotels were never an option because money was tight, and good relations were expressed by physical proximity and a willingness to help one another financially.

As they focused on the shared aspect of their values and recognized the influence of cultural norms, the couple's greater understanding facilitated their communication and problem solving. Although compromise was required on both parts, their relationship improved with their increased understanding of how and why each behaved as they did.

As in the case of Evelyn and John, many values are cross-cultural, but their expression differs. For example, intelligence is valued across cultures, but how one defines or expresses it differs significantly. In Western countries, thinking and responding quickly are core components (e.g., most of the tasks on the major intelligence tests are timed).

However, in many African countries, speed is less important than careful, deliberate thought and a large store of acquired knowledge. Similarly, wisdom is valued across cultures, but whereas a core expression of wisdom in Asian cultures is emotional restraint, it is not among European Americans. And most people value courage, but what is courageous in one culture may be considered foolhardy in another.

All cultures value communication as an essential part of human relations; however, norms vary regarding what information is appropriate to share, with whom, when, and how. Because the dominant culture often uses isolated examples to stereotype an entire group, sharing negative information about yourself, your family, or someone of your culture may be used against you or your culture. Similarly, many American Indian and Alaska Native people are reluctant to share information about traditional spiritual beliefs and sacred practices because such information has been misused and sold for profit by dominant-culture members.

Here is another exercise to get you thinking about how your values regarding privacy versus self-disclosure in communication may influence what, when, and how you communicate.

EXERCISE 10.2

Open Versus Private Communication[3]

For the first three categories of people, think of a specific person and write their first name in the blank spot under the categories of Friend, Family member, and Coworker. For the last person, imagine a stranger you meet on an airplane. Now for every item, put a check mark under each person's name with whom you'd feel comfortable sharing this information. For example, if you feel comfortable talking about your religious beliefs & practices only with the friend you named, put a check in the column under the friend's name but not under your family member's, coworker's, or the stranger columns.

(Continued)

[3]Inspired by *Public and Private Self* exercise in Pedersen, P. B. (2004). *110 experiences for multicultural learning* (pp. 96–98). Washington, DC: American Psychological Association; and *Taboo Topics Across Cultures* exercise in Goldstein, S. (2000). *Cross-cultural explorations: Activities in culture and psychology* (pp. 163–170). Needham Heights, MA: Allyn & Bacon.

(Continued)

	Friend	Family Member	Coworker	Stranger on airplane
Name:				
1. My religious beliefs and practices				
2. My political views				
3. My hurt feelings, re: this person				
4. My partner's gender				
5. How much money I make and have				
6. My views on racism and integration				
7. My psychological health				
8. My sex life				
9. My feelings about my body, weight				
10. My physical health				

Does the person's gender or culture make a difference in what you would share? Is there a difference between what you would share with a friend versus a family member? Are there some things you would never share at work, even with a work friend? Does it matter if the person is a stranger you will never see again?

There are people who would consider all the above topics to be private, and some who would feel comfortable sharing all this information with anyone. Whatever your preference, it is important to be aware that questions and information you consider benign could be perceived as invasive or insensitive by someone else. If a person is reluctant to talk about these or other areas, he or she may still value the relationship, but sharing this type of information is not a way he or she feels comfortable connecting. The more you learn about a person's culture, the more you will know when this is the case.

In sum, looking for different expressions of the same value creates an expectation of core similarities between people. This expectation facilitates a positive connection without denying the differences.

Step Back From Assumptions About Value Priorities

Crystal was a single, young Samoan woman who lived with her three young children and mother in a two-bedroom apartment. The family lived on Crystal's minimum-wage income and her mother's small Social Security disability check. Crystal's case manager (who was third-generation Mexican American) was helping her find a job that paid more, although he wanted her to enroll in college because he believed she was capable of obtaining a degree. No one in Crystal's family had ever gone to college and she did not appear interested, but the case manager thought her lack of interest reflected her lack of confidence that she could succeed.

The case manager struggled with his own desire to push Crystal to consider college. He was the first in his family to go to college and recognized the challenges involved, but he considered his life much better because he had obtained a degree. At the same time, he did not want to impose his own value priorities on Crystal, nor did he want her to feel "less than" if she did not go to college.

For helping professionals, the answer to such dilemmas is not easy, but consideration of value priorities can help. In this case, the case manager recognized that Crystal placed a higher value on having a job, in large part because of the expectation of her mother and extended family members who wanted her to have a job, at a time when she needed their support (i.e., when her children were small). The case manager focused on helping Crystal with her stated goal of finding a better job but continued to give her lots of positive feedback regarding her abilities, along with occasional college suggestions in the hope that he was building her self-confidence and planting a seed.

Power and Privilege to Consider

In a busy urban health clinic, the new receptionist (fourth-generation Latina American) had just helped an angry caller when a middle-aged, recently immigrated Sudanese woman came in and asked for a copy of her medical records. The receptionist explained that only the records clerk could give patients their records and she was out sick, but the receptionist would take the patient's address and have the clerk mail them. The patient had already requested her records by phone and thought she was being put off. Her voice became louder as she insisted she needed them that day. In response, the receptionist became patronizing in her tone. The argument grew until a supervisor intervened.

Power and privilege can be complex in their effects on interactions. In this case, although the receptionist and patient were both women of color, the receptionist was fourth-generation American and fluent in English, whereas the Sudanese woman had immigrated to the United States, was less familiar with clinic norms, and did not speak English fluently. The receptionist had a position of authority and thus greater privilege in relation to the patient, although she did not see herself as privileged because in the larger context of the clinic and dominant culture, she was not. Recognizing this power difference could have helped her engage with the patient in a more helpful way.

Empathize

A Christian student I will call Lisa told me the following story. Lisa was driving to class late, hurriedly looking for a parking spot, when she saw a man who appeared to be Middle Eastern pull his small car into two spots. The man got out of his car and laid his prayer mat out onto the second spot in front of his car, then kneeled down on the mat and began performing the Muslim prayers. As people drove by and saw him taking two parking spots, they began honking and yelling at him in anger, but he continued to pray. The student said she felt terrible for him. She said she was thinking how much strength it must take to follow one's religious calling to the point that other people become furious.

As Lisa told this story, I was moved by the compassion she showed for someone who was very different from her. The man was not of her own religion, *and* he had something she wanted (a parking spot). But she empathized with his spiritual intention to do the right thing, and in this way, she experienced a feeling of connection to the man.

This kind of situation is especially difficult to resolve because there is the perception that by one person getting what he wants, the other person loses something. However, if the opportunity had arisen to talk with this man about a better solution (e.g., putting his prayer mat on the sidewalk), Lisa would have been more able to engage with him than the angry, honking drivers whose judgmental attitude and angry behavior would have prevented problem solving.

Cultural Influences to Explore

Doug was a young White man who, after working with American Indian people in the large city where he grew up, decided to take a managerial position in health care with a Native organization in rural Alaska. Not long after he was hired, Doug became frustrated with what he considered the organization's slow pace. It seemed to him that even when a change would benefit everyone, the decision had to be discussed in so many formats by so many people that it took forever.

Doug knew that he was the only person who felt this way, so he talked with a trusted coworker who helped him to see another perspective. The coworker emphasized the organization's common goal (which Doug shared) of helping community members in need and explained how important it was for everyone to feel valued in their work, in part because it was so hard to find qualified staff in a rural area. By seeking consensus whenever possible, the tribal leaders showed that they valued everyone's input into potential change, and consensus eliminated conflicts that might occur afterwards without it.

As Doug thought more about the influence of culture on his assumptions of what was best, he recognized that he had always lived in a high-tech, urban area where "asap" was the baseline expectation for any project. He could see that there were pros and cons to both approaches and began to appreciate how the slower pace allowed for more relaxed and enjoyable social interactions between people.

Think Differently

During conflicts, there is a tendency to assume that one's own value priorities are the best, especially when those priorities are supported by the dominant culture. The language used to think and talk about values reflects this bias. Often, the thought is "I hold this (positive) value and you don't." Then the other person's value priority is described in negative terms. For example, "I value independence and you don't. You are dependent/codependent/enmeshed with your family." Can you hear how the latter terms are polar opposites and judgmental in tone?

One way to counter such negative assumptions is by looking for a positive term to describe the other person's priority. To use the same example, the person might say to himself or herself, "I place a high priority on independence, and you place a higher priority on interde-pendence." Note that the term *interdependence* does not have a pejora-tive connotation.

This reframing recognizes that just because someone prioritizes one value does not mean he or she completely denies the importance of the other value. Highly independent people are still interdependent on some level to survive, and more interdependent people still want some personal autonomy. The difference is mainly one of emphasis.

Table 10.2   Reframing Judgmental Assumptions

Judgmental: I value equality and egalitarian interactions, and you do not. You prefer an authoritarian approach.
Reframe: While I value egalitarian interactions, your priority is on demonstrating respect, which recognizes an individual's greater knowledge, experience, and authority.
Judgmental: I value openness, and you are closed.
Reframe: I value openness, and you are cautious, show good self-control, and are more reserved.
Judgmental: I value change, and you are resistant.
Reframe: I value change, and you place a higher value on patience.
Judgmental: I value hard work, and you are lazy.
Reframe: I value hard work, and in your culture or country, working harder may be pointless because it does not lead to greater pay or advancement.
Judgmental: I value honesty, and you are dishonest.
Reframe: I value honesty, and you value harmonious relationships, which may require not sharing everything one thinks.
Judgmental: I value action, and you resign yourself to fate.
Reframe: I value action, and you place a higher priority on patience and acceptance.
Judgmental: I value competition, and you give up easily/don't try hard enough.
Reframe: I place a higher value on competition, and you place a higher priority on cooperation and acceptance.

EXERCISE 10.3

Practicing Respectful Resolution

Think of a value you hold strongly. Now think of someone who frustrates you and who you think does not hold this value. Remember the RESPECT strategies:

Recognize a shared or similar value.

Expression of the same value may differ, so think about this.

Step back from assumptions about value priorities and what is right.

Power—Consider differences of power and privilege.

Empathize—Look for compassionate, nonjudgmental explanations.

Culture—Consider its influence on behavior, views, and beliefs—yours and others'.

Think differently—Use language to positively reframe others' value priorities.

Using one of these strategies, try to think about this person in a way that decreases your negative feelings and increases your openness to him or her. If you have the opportunity, use the strategy to help you resolve, minimize, or avoid conflict with this person. If the strategy doesn't work, try another one.

11

Conclusion

Knowledge that takes you not beyond yourself is far worse than ignorance.

—Sufi saying[1]

Unlike the subjects we learned once in school, relationships require a lifetime of learning. What makes this learning challenging is the continually changing nature of the information we need. In an effort to understand this learning process, psychologist Steven Regeser López[2] asked counselors in a multicultural training course to chronicle their experiences. Afterward, he and the student-counselors combed through the data and found four common stages to their learning.

In the first stage, counselors showed a lack of awareness of cultural influences on themselves and on their clients and relationships. Counselors did not believe they had any biases and experienced no distress about their lack of cross-cultural competence, because they did not perceive culture to be important.

---

[1]Quoted by Elif Shafak in her TED talk, July 2010. Retrieved from www.elifshafak.com/ted_eng.asp

[2]López, S. R., Grover, K. P., Holland, D., Johnson, M. J., Kain, C. D., Kanel, K., Mellins, C. A., & Rhyne, M. C. (1989). Development of culturally sensitive psychotherapists. *Professional Psychology: Research and Practice, 20,* 369–376.

In the second stage, as counselors began learning cultural information, they started noticing cultural influences on themselves, including personal biases. They began considering cultural explanations for clients' beliefs and behaviors; however, these explanations were often based on stereotypes. Counselors reported an increased appreciation for diversity but also began experiencing frustration with the challenges involved.

In the third stage, counselors reported increasing confusion and frustration as awareness of their own limitations grew. The need to consider cultural influences without a clear understanding of those influences was perceived as more of a burden than a help. Counselors experienced more ambivalence and defensiveness in their work with clients who were culturally different from themselves.

In the fourth stage, described as one of *synthesis,* counselors were aware of their own biases but more accepting of their need to continue learning on an ongoing basis. They showed an ability to think about and use cultural information flexibly and to adapt this information to each client's needs and preferences. In this stage, counselors reported increased appreciation of the richness involved in working with diverse people.

In my own work training counselors and psychologists, there is one additional quality I have observed during the synthesis stage. As people learn about privilege, "isms," and unfairness in the world, they often feel a desire to go beyond the individual level of relationships to changing organizations and society. Such advocacy and social justice work can take a variety of forms—for example, the brother of a young gay man becomes active in PFLAG (Parents and Friends of Lesbians and Gays); parents of a child born with cerebral palsy become advocates for increased rights for people with disabilities; a young woman decides after receiving an MBA to teach finance classes to communities of people living in poverty; an educator decides to use his social connections to raise funds to build a school for girls in another country.

Keep in mind that people do not always move through these stages in a linear way, and a high level of cultural competence with one group does not ensure competence with another. For example, a young White lesbian woman may have a high level of awareness, knowledge, and skill in working with sexual minorities who are White, but need a great deal more learning to understand the experiences of lesbian and gay people of color. A Latino Christian man may form great relationships with Christian Whites and people of color but have a limited understanding of Jews, Muslims, Hindus, and Buddhists. It is most helpful to think of these stages as culture specific and variable.

Hopefully, wherever you are now is further along than when you began reading this book. If you began in Stage 1 regarding a particular minority culture and now find yourself in a second or third stage, you may be feeling more frustrated. But if you continue learning and watching out for defensiveness that can cut you off from people and new ideas, it will get better. If your journey has taken you to the synthesis stage with regard to a particular culture, I hope you will continue to expand your experiences to cultures that are new to you. There is never a shortage of cultures to learn from, and cross-cultural relationships offer unique possibilities for personal growth, friendship, success, and making a difference.

EXERCISE 11.1

Reflection Questions

1. What is the most significant thing you have learned about building cross-cultural relationships? How could this new information help you?

2. What is the most significant thing you have learned about *yourself* with regard to cross-cultural relationships? How could this insight help you?

3. What is your biggest strength in building cross-cultural relationships? How can you reinforce this strength, build upon it, and/or make the most of it?

4. What is your biggest weakness when it comes to building cross-cultural relationships? What can you do to counter or minimize this weakness?

References

Adler, A. (1938/2011). *Social interest: A challenge to mankind.* Eastford, CT: Martino Fine Books.

Alexie, S. (1993). *The Lone Ranger and Tonto fistfight in heaven.* New York: Grove Press.

American religion identification survey. (2008). Retrieved from http://commons .trincoll.edu/aris/6

Ashrif, S. (1987). Eurocentrism and myopia in science teaching. *Multicultural Teaching, 5,* 28–30.

Berry, J. W., Poortinga, Y. H., Segall, M. H., & Dasen, P. R. (1992). *Cross-cultural psychology: Research and applications.* New York: Cambridge University Press.

Bronson, P., & Merryman, A. (2009). *NutureShock.* New York: Twelve/Hachette Book Group.

Comas-Díaz, L. (2011). *Multicultural care: A clinician's guide to cultural competence.* Washington, DC: American Psychological Association.

Crimmins, C. (2004). *How the homosexuals saved civilization.* New York: Penguin.

Dalai Lama, & Cutler, H. C. (2009). *The art of happiness in a troubled world.* New York: Doubleday.

Davis, K. (2005). *A girl like me.* Retrieved from www.youtube.com/watch?v= Wk_x7s3QiYk

Department of Housing and Urban Development. (2008). *FAIR HOUSING— PART 2: Interesting statistics* (2008 Annual Report). Retrieved from http:// petriestocking.com/blog/2009/07/10/fair-housing-part-2-interesting- statistics-from-huds-2008-annual-report/

Fiske, S. (1993). Controlling other people: The impact of power on stereotyping. *American Psychologist, 48,* 621–628.

Gallardo, E. (2006, January 16). Batchelet next Chilean president. *Peninsula Clarion,* p. A-7.

Gates, H. L. Jr. (2011). *Black in Latin America.* New York: New York University Press.

Goldstein, S. (2000). *Cross-cultural explorations: Activities in culture and psychology.* Needham Heights, MA: Allyn & Bacon.

Greene, B. (2009). The use and abuse of religious beliefs in dividing and conquering between socially marginalized groups: The same-sex marriage debate. *American Psychologist, 64,* 698–709.

Griffin-Pierce, T. (1997). When I am lonely the mountains call me: The impact of sacred geography on Navajo psychological well-being. *American Indian and Alaskan Native Mental Health Research, 7,* 1–10.

Hays, P. A. (2008). *Addressing cultural complexities in practice: Assessment, diagnosis, and therapy.* Washington, DC: American Psychological Association.

Hill, M. (2009). I didn't always wear a tuxedo. In D. Savage & T. Miller (Eds.), *It gets better: Coming out, overcoming bullying, and creating a life worth living* (pp. 201–206). New York: Dutton.

Kawagley, O. (1995). *A Yupiaq worldview: A pathway to ecology and spirit.* Prospect Heights, IL: Waveland Press.

Klontz, B., Klontz, T., & Kahler, R. (2008). *Wired for wealth.* Deerfield Park, IL: Health Communications.

Lawrence-Lightfoot, S. (2000). *Respect.* Cambridge, MA: Perseus Books.

López, S. R., Grover, K. P., Holland, D., Johnson, M. J., Kain, C. D., Kanel, K., Mellins, C. A., & Rhyne, M. C. (1989). Development of culturally sensitive psychotherapists. *Professional Psychology: Research and Practice, 20,* 369–376.

Lumumba-Kasongo, M. (2006, April 3). My black skin makes my white coat vanish. *Newsweek, 147*(14), 20.

Matheson, L. (1986). If you are not an Indian, how do you treat an Indian? In H. P. Lefley & P. Pedersen (Eds.), *Cross-cultural training for mental health professionals* (pp. 115–130). Springfield, IL: Charles C Thomas.

McIntosh, P. (1998). White privilege and male privilege. In M. L. Andersen & P. Hill Collins (Eds.), *Race, class and gender* (3rd ed., pp. 94–105). Belmont, CA: Wadsworth.

Mona, L. R., Romessner-Scehnet, J. M., Cameron, R. P., & Cardenas, V. (2006). Cognitive-Behavior therapy and people with disabilities. In P. A. Hays & G. Y. Iwamasa (Eds.), *Culturally responsive cognitive-behavioral therapy: Assessment, practice, and supervision* (pp. 199–222). Washington, DC: American Psychological Association.

National Organization of Women. (2011). Retrieved from www.now.org/issues.affirm/talking.html

Novas, H. (1994). *Everything you need to know about Latino history.* New York: Penguin.

Olkin, R. (1999). *What psychotherapists should know about disability.* New York: Guilford Press.

Palsson, J. (2008, December).10 famous people with disabilities. *ArticleDoctor.* Retrieved from www.articledoctor.com/disability/10-famous-people-disabilities-581

Payne, R. K. (1996*). A framework for understanding poverty* (3rd ed.). Highlands, TX: Aha! Process.

Pedersen, P. B. (1997). *Culture-centered counseling interventions: Striving for accuracy.* Thousand Oaks, CA: Sage.

Pedersen, P. B. (2004). *110 experiences for multicultural learning*. Washington, DC: American Psychological Association.

Prince, S. (2010, November 30). What's in your knapsack [Web message]? Retrieved from blog http://therapeuticjustice.blogspot.com/2010/11/whats-in-your-knapsack.html

Richman, J. (1999). Psychotherapy with the suicidal elderly: A family-oriented approach. In M. Duffy (Ed.), *Handbook of counseling and psychotherapy with older adults* (pp. 650–661). New York: Wiley.

Roberts Potts, R. (2011). Dear Uncle Ronnie. In D. Savage & T. Miller (Ed.), *It gets better: Coming out, overcoming bullying, and creating a life worth living* (pp. 183–184). New York: Dutton/Penguin.

Rochlin, M. (1977). *The heterosexual questionnaire*. Retrieved from www.pflag westchester.org/PrideWorks/2008_Handouts/HeterosexualQuestionnaire .pdf

Smith, H. (1991). *The world's religions*. New York: HarperCollins.

Spickard, P. R. (1992). The illogic of racial categories. In M. P. P. Root (Ed.), *Racially mixed people in America* (pp. 12–23). Newbury Park, CA: Sage.

Stewart, J. C. (1996). *1001 things you should know about African American history*. New York: Broadway Books.

Sue, D. W., Capodilupo, C. M., Torino, G. C., Bucceri, J. M., Holder, A. M. B., Nadal, K. L., & Esquilin, M. (2007). Racial microaggressions in everyday life. *American Psychologist, 62*, 271–286.

Swan-Reimer, C. (1999). *Counseling the Inupiat Eskimo*. Westport, CT: Greenwood Press.

U.S. Bureau of Labor Statistics. (2001). Table A-2. Employment status of the civilian population by race, sex, and age. Retrieved from www.bls.gov/news.release/empsit.t02.htm

U.S. Census Bureau. (2000). 20th anniversary of Americans with Disabilities Act. Retrieved from www.census.gov/newsroom/releases/archives/facts_for_features_special_editions/cb10-ff13.html

U.S. Census Bureau. (2005–2009). *New Census Bureau report analyzes nation's linguistic diversity* (American Community Survey). Retrieved from www .census.gov/newsroom/releases/archives/american_community_survey_ acs/cb10-cn58.html

U.S. Census Bureau. (2010). Older Americans month. Retrieved from www.census.gov/newsroom/releases/archives/facts_for_features_ special_editions/cb10-ff06.html

U.S. Census Bureau. (2011). *2010 shows America's diversity* (American Community Survey). Retrieved from http://2010.census.gov/news/releases/operations/ cb11-cn125.html

Williams, C. B. (1999). Claiming a biracial identity: Resisting social constructions of race and culture. *Journal of Counseling & Development, 77*, 32–35.

Index

About the Author

Pamela A. Hays is author of the book *Addressing Cultural Complexities in Practice* and co-editor of *Culturally Responsive Cognitive-Behavioral Therapy.* She holds a PhD in clinical psychology from the University of Hawaii and from 1987 to 1988, served as NIMH Postdoctoral Fellow at the University of Rochester School of Medicine. From 1989 to 2000, she worked as a core faculty member of the graduate psychology program at Antioch University Seattle, where she continues to teach once a year as adjunct. Her research has included work with Vietnamese, Lao, and Cambodian people living in the United States and with Arab Muslim women living in North Africa. Since 2000, she has been back in her hometown of Soldotna, Alaska, working in private practice and as a supervisor for the Kenaitze Tribe's Nakenu Family Center in Kenai, Alaska. She conducts workshops internationally and can be reached at www.drpamelahays.com.

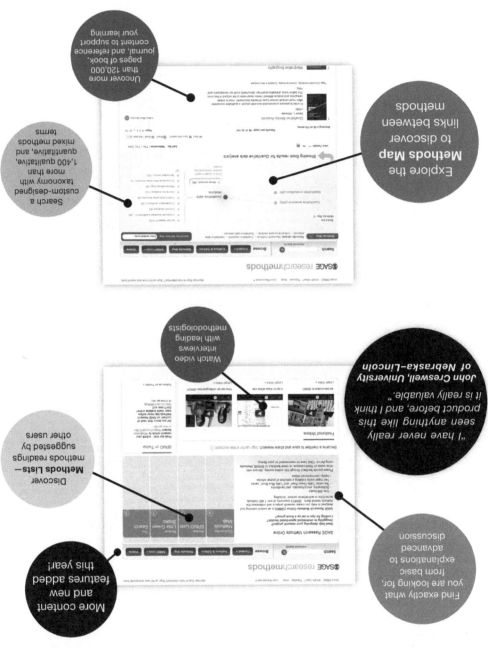